Charlie's Paradise,
1967-68

CHARLIE'S PARADISE, 1967–68

Michael Vitel

Best Wishes + God Bless

Michael Vitel

VANTAGE PRESS
New York / Atlanta
Los Angeles / Chicago

Published by Vantage Press, Inc.
516 West 34th Street, New York, New York 10001

Manufactured in the United States of America
ISBN: 0-533-06980-7

Library of Congress Catalog Card No.: 86-90026

SECOND EDITION 2005
Ideal Printing Co.
420 - 31st Street N., St. Petersburg, FL 33713

THIRD EDITION 2020
Florida Print Solutions
432 - 31st Street N., St. Petersburg, FL 33713

To the marines,
who will never be forgotten

Foreword

This is a true story!

It came from the diary of a nineteen-year-old typical American boy who lived through thirteen months of the hell that was Vietnam.

It shows it all, the good, the bad, and the ugly, just as he experienced it.

The heroic side is there—buddies risking lives to shelter other buddies.

Courage is there, and dogged persistence overcoming danger from the enemies and ever-present mud and filth.

Loneliness of a boy reading and rereading the letters from home is there.

The horror and suspense of nights in a foxhole with shells falling oh-so-close is there. The wondering, over and over: *why am I here? Does anyone care?*

It was painful for Mike to relive it all. It will be painful to read and remember.

Maybe it will help our resolve to prevent sending more typical American boys to be reluctant heroes on distant shores again.

Glenn J. Cook

Preface

This book takes you on a journey with Mike Vichelli from the time he made a big decision, to the training it caused him to undergo and later to the heart of Charlie's Paradise, better known to the public as Vietnam. The book tells of the men he served with, the ones he laughed with, the ones he prayed with. It tells about the many marines who had so much to live for and who died for so little. The places Vichelli takes you through won't be all in battle; there were great places, fun places, and places to be content. Mike gets involved with things that at one time would have seemed unreal.

Mike's a well-liked marine, and when somebody gets tight with him, he's more than just a buddy. Whenever one of his buddies was killed in action, a part of him also died. It was that much harder to carry on. The story will begin in the year of 1966 and take the reader up to early spring in '68. The book ends there, but for Mike Vichelli, life was about to start over.

Charlie's Paradise, 1967-68

Chapter I

It was the summer of 1966, and I was holding down a job at the First National Bank of Chicago. It was an ordinary job, in an ordinary city, and I was living an ordinary life, in an ordinary town. The army had been sending letters to me, wanting me, Mike Vichelli, to register for the draft. Being almost nineteen now, I knew I'd have to be going very shortly. I wasn't in a very big hurry, because I had only been out of high school a year. My older brother, Chuck Vichelli, was already in the army, with four hard years of college behind him. Both of us were hard workers, but we still were very different. With Chuck, studying came first, which didn't leave him much time to get in trouble or, as I called it, have fun. Although I was a hard worker, I played hard, too. Chuck had some of his goals set, being older and more wiser, as they say. When it came to me, it was just the opposite. I didn't know what I wanted.

The months passed, and I grew restless. I heard of my friends who were signing up for the marines. Some were already in. I didn't want to hold out any longer and, once again not following in my brother's footsteps, I chose to join the marines. I signed the papers and took the 120-day program before actually reporting to basic training.

Shortly after that, I took a leave of absence from my job and let the time pass away. I didn't wait the full 120 days, and I'm really not sure why. I guess I just wanted to get it over with. Now a private, I took my oath and left on the same day for MCRD, San Diego, California. Every-

1

thing was moving fast for the thirty-one boys from Illinois, and it really began when the groups of boys arrived early in the morning for their basic training. Yes, I said boys, but the ones that made it through basic wouldn't be boys when it was over.

The harassment and the discipline started immediately, by having us fellows stand at attention on some yellow footprints. Some of the fellows didn't know if this was going to be for real, but it was. They marched four or five of us in at a time and began cutting off all our hair—more like shaving our heads! Now that no one looked the same, we thought that we might be able to get some sleep and forget what had happened. Brother, were we wrong! The drill instructors, better known as the DIs and also as. . . well, we'll forget that part, marched us over to another building, to get some different clothing, including our utility uniforms.

We were going to know these uniforms really well before this was over. The boys hit the sack, but before any dreams were finished, a new day was starting. The days passed and we began to hate our DIs even more. We were called quite a few different names in boot camp, but some I'd rather not repeat. The trainees put in a sixteen-hour day seven days a week. The platoon was made up of eighty-five fellows, but only seventy-six graduated. The other nine couldn't make the grind. The training was rugged, and we learned a lot, especially how to be bitter. The skinny got built up; the fat boys were trimmed down.

The times we weren't running our heads off, we had classes, and we were taught everything by the book, and what isn't in the book we learned the hard way. It didn't take long to learn that we never call our rifle a gun. Our gun was used for something else, in fact a much greater use once we pulled liberty. As the training went on, so did the classes. We learned drownproofing, the history of the marine corps, the articles, cleanliness (all over again), and much more. I took good notes, like some of the others, but there were some that just wanted to get by with as little effort as they could. I wanted to be a good marine, but I also knew if these notes could save my life, I would make them a part of myself. No matter how bad things got, I didn't want to go to the island in the sky. In drownproofing, we learned full light inflation, and how to use the water for support. Slow, easy movements, extreme relaxation. For every inch you come out of the water, you will go down a foot. You must conserve your energy. I learned to use my clothing to retain body heat or to make a life jacket. Our instructor ended the class by telling us that one out of five people drowned in Vietnam. This started us thinking!

When it came to learning more about our rifle, it was brought to our attention that the M-14, unloaded, weighed nine pounds. The fully loaded weight is eleven pounds. Overall length is forty-four inches, the length of the barrel is twenty-two inches, and the chamber pressure is 50,000 pounds per square inch. The speed of the bullet muzzle velocity is 2,800 feet per second. The maximum range is 3,725 meters. This was all very interesting information about our rifle, but at this time many of us were thinking about when we would have to use it for the first time in combat. We faced facts, because we all knew where we would likely end up after our training was complete.

The training got tougher, but the classes got better and longer. The drill instructors considered the classes important, even though they enjoyed harassing us. This particular class was on the code of conduct, and it was important that we learn it and learn it good.

Of the 4,428 Americans who survived communist imprisonment after the Korean War, 192 were found chargeable with serious offenses against fellow servicemen and country. As a result of this, the United States Armed Forces were given the following code of conduct:

Article 1: I am an American fighting man. I serve in the forces which guard my country and its way of life. I am prepared to give my life in its defense.

Article 2: I will never surrender of my own free will. If in command, I will never surrender my men while they still have means to resist.

Article 3: If I am captured, I will continue to resist by all means available. I will make every effort to escape and aid others to escape. I will accept neither parole nor special favors from the enemy.

Article 4: If I become a prisoner of war, I will keep faith with my fellow prisoners. I will give no information nor take part in any action which might be harmful to my comrades. If I am senior, I will take command. If not, I will obey the lawful orders of those appointed over me and will back them up in every way.

Article 5: When questioned, should I become a prisoner of war, I am bound to give only name, rank, service number, and date of birth. I will evade answering further questions to the utmost of my ability. I will make no oral or written statements disloyal to my country and its allies or harmful to their cause.

Article 6: I will never forget that I am an American fighting man, responsible for my actions and dedicated to the principles which made my country free. I will trust in my God and in the United States of America.

The instructor went on to tell us that the articles are not meant to teach us to become a prisoner of war. They are meant to guide us in our conduct if, after doing everything in our power to prevent it, we become a prisoner of war. The code is intended to make us realize that the prison camp is an extension of the battlefield.

As we were sitting on the bleachers and the class was nearing its end, a marine raised his hand and asked the instructor what reason we had for being in Vietnam. Even though we were to learn more about our goal and reasons later, the instructor gave us the following reasons at this time. He said there were many reasons and one might be economical. Another was to unify Vietnam. He explained that there is a lot of war because Vietnam is coming out of the dark ages. Our actions and what we do there were very important, almost as important as killing Cong. If the people were on on our side, the Vietcong wouldn't have anywhere to hide. We must win the hearts and minds of the average Vietcong. They would be for us and help us all they could.

The weeks slipped past, and by this time every recruit was totally homesick. We were nearing the seventh week of inspection, and the platoon had really started to shape up. The harassment wasn't as great now, because the DIs were running out of time, trying to get us ready for the second phase of training. The seventy-six recruits that made it this far were not about to give up. A lot of the training now was repeated, over and over, like shaping the finish on a fine piece of artwork. We felt like men now, and we could see the difference; we didn't have to be told.

The time had finally come to graduate, and the ceremony took place in the beautiful camp theater. It was the first time anyone had called us marines, and it came from the general in charge of MCRD. We were given a copy of his speech, and I'd like to quote it, if I may:

"To you as future marines, welcome aboard. You young men are citizens of the strongest nation on this earth, the United States of America. You, and people like you, are the reason for that strength. Individually, you may be physically weak, but from this day on and each succeeding day during your training, you must dedicate yourself to becoming physically strong, mentally awake, and morally strong, so that you will be able to do your part in keeping your country strong and free. We Americans, you and I, our fathers and mothers, and all of our loved ones, must be thankful for the strength and freedom of our country. But being thankful is not enough. Our freedoms were hard won, and it is our job to protect them.

"Why, I ask, do we have so many freedoms and such a great American way of life? It is the result of the hard work of honest, dedicated people who have made this nation a great democracy. Marines before you have died fighting to protect it and to keep it free, to keep it a land where all men are created free. Many of your parents, and their parents before them, your relatives and friends, have done something to help make this country great. You—each and every one of you—must now do your part honestly and faithfully.

"When you enlisted, you raised your right hand and swore that you would bear true faith and allegiance to the United States of America, and that you would serve them honestly and faithfully against all their enemies whomsoever. This is a sacred oath taken by you of your own free will and there is a great trust placed in you by the people of America, that you honor your oath. If you are to be a United States marine, you will honor your oath—cherish it as only free Americans can—and fulfill it—both in spirit and letter.

"The marines' motto is *Semper Fidelis*. Its meaning is this: *Always faithful*—faithful to yourself, your comrades. You were here, and we tried to teach you the real meaning of this motto. We intended to teach you what you had to know if you were to be a marine, a member of the finest fighting force in the world. Thank you."

I thought about the words I had read the first day I arrived for basic training. The plaque on the wall says that the training is going to be tough: "It has to be in order for the Marine Corps to maintain its unbeatable reputation. Always remember, hundreds of thousands of other young men have gone through recruit training; you will be a basic marine when you complete the training. You, your family, and your friends will be proud of the fact that you completed this phase of your Marine Corps career. The treatment you will receive here will be different from that which you have been used to. It will be hard for you, but it will be fair. Many men have passed and many men will follow you through these doors to success." I was still daydreaming when this big son of a bitch bumped my arm and said, "Move out, marine."

Everyone was in a hurry to leave the theater, because we had some free time before returning to our squad bays to pick up our orders. The big guy walked behind me until we got outside, and then he asked me what the hell I was thinking about. I told him, "A lot of things," and let it go at that. He told me his name was Bruce Largo, so I introduced myself and kept walking toward the PX to get something to eat. Bruce was headed there also, and you didn't have to be smart to know that this guy must be a big eater. I didn't mind the company, but I couldn't help thinking about leaving tomorrow. I remembered seeing Bruce a few times during our basic training, but we were in different platoons, so I never really met him. After we had something to eat, we headed back to pick up our orders and get a lot of things ready for leaving this place. Since we were from different areas on the base, we shook hands, figuring maybe we'll see each other tomorrow before we leave, or maybe never again.

When I got back to the squad bay, it dawned on me that Bruce and I never even discussed what state we were from. Oh well, it was too late now, and I wanted to pack and see what my orders were and get some sleep. In that order.

Chapter II

The next morning took forever to come, because I knew that later that evening I would be home for thirty glorious days, including Christmas, with the family.

The time had finally come. We were all standing at attention in our dress green uniforms. After a few words from our platoon commander and DIs, we were dismissed. Now it was up to us to find our own way home. It was hard to believe that our training for now was over. This was only a part of it, though. I glanced once more at my orders; then I shoved them into the folder and got on the bus. The bus was taking us to the airport, but some of the other marines' folks came to pick them up. These lucky fellows would be home in less than an hour.

All the while I was at the airport and all the way on the plane, I was thinking of the many things I had to do. The trick was going to be getting them done in thirty days. I met my folks at O'Hare Airport, and what a welcome sight they were. Everyone looked real good and I couldn't wait to show my little brother Greg what I had for him. It was the Marine Corps dress blue uniform. My hometown buddy Ray Richilew was also there, and I noticed the change the Marine Corps had done for him. He had been in the marines almost a year now, but had three long years to go. I myself had only enlisted for three years.

When we arrived at the house, I unloaded my gear and talked with the folks awhile before Ray and I took off for some of the local pubs. It was great driving around town again, and my folks were very understanding about my being on the go. I was given my dad's car just about every time I needed it.

My folks would have liked me to stay home more but never stopped me from doing what I wanted to do. Maybe they thought I had earned the right. I know I certainly thought I had.

Every day something was planned. I went back to the bank to visit and also went to some of the old hangouts. When I wasn't at a lounge or tavern with Ray, I was taking in a movie with some girl. I wasn't serious about any girl, so the more I took them out, the more I missed being home.

Every time I wanted the clock to stop, it seemed the days went by faster. It was nearing the end of my leave, and I knew that next year I wouldn't be home for Christmas or New Year's. My folks had a feeling I would be going overseas, but I knew for sure I would be going over soon.

As I look back on my thirty days at home, I can't help but wonder what time will do to some of the girls I met and to some of the places I'd been to. Some of the girls will have gotten married, places will have closed up or changed owners, and the crowds that used to go there will not be the same. However, the one thing that won't change is the love my folks have for me. If nothing else, that alone will help me get back.

I met a lot of nice girls and even though I didn't have much time to get serious with any of them, it made leaving that much harder. Of course, I won't forget Linda, Judy, Kathy, and so on.

I bought myself a little black diary and began filling up the pages with my feelings from day to day. As I look back, the first couple of pages went something like this. "This is my diary! I hope to finish it! This will cover my pre-training and my term in Vietnam. It starts from my last day with my family, and I hope it goes until the day

I fly home. I'm going to be scared, but I hope that what I am doing will be for a worthy cause. Thirteen months is a hell of a long time. I'm going to miss everyone and everything.

"This book will go everywhere I go, and the only way someone will read this is if I'm not there to stop them."

That was the first two pages, and at that time, I never thought that someday I would be telling this to the public.

Now it was January, 1967. It was also Sunday, New Year's Day! I was spending the last day with my family, and I was really feeling bad about leaving. I was thankful that I got to be home for Christmas and New Year's, but it still hurt knowing I'd miss next year. My dad sat around in his pajamas; my mom made bacon and eggs, trying to hold back the tears. Little Greg really didn't know what was going on, and my sister Joyce, well, she had her own worries. As for brother Chuck and sister Carol, they were both married and doing okay.

Even though it was cold outside, I wanted to get out and get my mind off leaving. I borrowed my dad's car, like so many other times, and started using up gas. I played the radio a lot, always loud too. My dad always said, "It wears down the battery, especially in winter." I thought to myself, with my being gone, it was sure to last another winter.

When I stopped at a store in LaGrange Park, I met a girl I used to go to school with. Her name was Sandy, and she looked real good to me, as good as a girl could look when you're leaving the next morning. Towards evening I spent some quiet hours with her, but left early to get started packing for the next day. I didn't know it then, but Sandy was to be the last girl I'd see from Illinois for over fourteen months.

The next morning we left early, and it was rougher

leaving than when I left for boot camp. My folks drove me to the airport to see me off. It was nice to have them there, but it made it twice as hard on me. Once inside the plane, I was still able to see them, even though they couldn't see me any longer. I wish I had a dollar for every tear I dropped that day.

Chapter III

The plane ride was comfortable, and I got back to Basic Infantry School the same day. I reported in right away, because that's the way I am. I don't like being late. That would only upset the sergeants more than they were already. They assigned me to a barracks and I got to pick out what bunk I wanted.

Whenever I could, I always picked out a top bunk. It seemed no matter how you try, the bottom bunk would always get messed. Some marines would always be sitting on it, or the guy on top would step on it when he was going up and down from his bunk.

It was getting late, so I unpacked and cleaned up. I hopped up into the sack and stared up at the ceiling. I said to myself, "Am I ready for this? Starting tomorrow I'm in for three hard weeks of mortar school." At that time, the sergeant yelled, "Lights out." We all thought training would start early, but actually it won't start until tomorrow. We didn't do very much today, except stand in line after line drawing our 782 gear. Now, 782 gear is everything a marine might or will use in the field. It includes canteens, a cartridge belt, eating utensils, packs, a helmet, rain gear, et cetera.

The day seemed to drag by and no one would fill us in on what to expect on Wednesday. I had a lot of time left before the lights went out, so I sat down and wrote a few letters. I also started thinking about the good times I left behind. Most of the fellows, including myself, just hated the thought of training all over again.

The days flew by and before we knew it, we were already studying for our first exam. Every day was more of the same, more lectures, more classes. I studied hard, because I wanted to know what was going on. Where we were going, a guy needed every edge he could get.

Well, the studying paid off, at least for the first test. I scored a ninety and I was damn glad that week was over.

It was now Saturday, January 7, and some of us lucky fellows were off on liberty. I took off for Disneyland with James Dinn—what a weekend that was. Jim was from California and he sure knew where to go for some action. I heard a lot about Disneyland when I was kid watching "The Mickey Mouse Club," but now I got to see it for the first time. It didn't mean as much to Jim as it did to me, probably because Jim had been there more times than he could count. No matter what we went there for, I had a good time and the place was everything people said about it. When we were leaving Disneyland, Jim asked if I wanted to spend the rest of the weekend with his folks. He knew I had no special plans, and he probably had this figured from the beginning. I felt good about that, and I guess I hoped it would turn out like that all along.

I met Jim for the first time at the beginning of our mortar training. We had the top bunks next to each other and seemed to hit it off fine. Neither one of us had any special girl waiting for us, and we also didn't know what we wanted out of life. The other thing we had in common was that we enjoyed having some good times. The weekend was over and I thanked Jim for having me stay in a great place. His parents treated me real well and this is something I will not forget.

The next day we were back in training and learning more and more about the mortars. The training never seemed to end, and then came our second test. The day of the test I scored only a seventy-five and we fired the mortars for the first time. They sure were some noisy bastards, if you didn't hold your ears.

I felt myself getting lazy during this part of the training, and I knew it was a bad feeling. It happened other times, and it's not good. Someone usually gets hurt when this feeling occurs. Our third test was coming up, and I wanted to score well to bring up my average. It wouldn't really matter unless a guy didn't get a passing grade, but still I didn't like getting a seventy-five on my last test.

The day of the third test came, and I surprised myself and scored a ninety-five. We fired the mortars for the second time in our training. The days passed, and we were still training and still firing the mortars. All this was leading up to the gunner's test. Now let me tell you something: I probably had butterflies in my stomach from the beginning of my enlistment, but times like this they started flying around.

It was now January 14, Saturday, another weekend away from training. Jim had to go to a party of some kind, so I took off with Sam Munuchy. Sam was also from California and, like Jim, knew the hot spots for tourists like me. We ended up at Knotts' Berry Farm, which wasn't bad at all for our purposes. I was still with Sam the next day. We had dinner at his girl's house, and once again I was treated very well. We also spent some more time at Knotts' Berry Farm, since Sam lived so close by it.

It came that time again to take the lousy ride back to the base.

The next morning the sergeants ran us through our gunner's test, and no matter what kind of weekend we had, everyone in the platoon did very well. It goes to show you what a little training can do.

We were also trained on the 60 mortars, just in case

there were no openings in the 81s when we got where we were going. We took a quick gunner's test on these and started preparing for our final exam.

It was now only our eleventh day of training. It was this day that we took our final exam. I scored a seventy-six. It sure wasn't the best score, but then again, I wasn't the best marine.

At this point, our training with the mortars was over. All we had left to do was fire the .45 caliber pistol and turn in our 782 gear. Next week someone else would be wearing this crap. After our gear was turned in, the sergeant permitted us to go back to begin packing for Staging Battalion. You guessed it, more training!

The day we outposted was Friday, January 20. We were really glad to leave. We also got paid, which made us even happier.

We arrived at Mainside, California, and they began checking us in right away. The first thing we heard was that no liberty went for the weekend. All this money on us, and we couldn't get off the base. One marine made a common joke out of it. He said maybe they'll start our training right now, so we get the war over a few days earlier. We were given base liberty, so we went to the club and got drunk on our ass.

By this time I didn't see too much of James Dinn. At the end of our last training, things got pretty hectic, and we were not together much. When he didn't come around, I figured he got hung up on some broad and really started seeing her on weekends. If anything, broads will make some guys forget about everything.

It was Sunday, and Sam and I were recovering from our hangovers. We were still stuck on base, so Sam called his girl and his buddy. They came down, and we spent the day at the hostess house. It rained like a bitch all day.

The training started right up and all over again. This time it was a processing stage, to get us ready for Okinawa. Okinawa was to be our last stop before we entered Charlie's Paradise.

It was our first day of processing, so they gave us some shots, and then we did some PT. Everyone knows what that is: physical training. In the next couple of days we were to draw our 782 gear again and move to a place called Las Pulgas. It could easily be called Lost Persons if you were to slip off the mountains. This place had mountains higher than any I had ever seen.

We started training as soon as we got there, and we had our battle sights put on our rifles. This is the elevation we go by in firing our weapons. It varies from time to time. Later in the evening we had a rifle inspection.

Saturday somehow slipped up on the platoon commanders, and before they knew it, liberty call had arrived. Since Sam and I were still together in the same squad bays, he asked me to come home with him again. By this time, we were pretty damn good friends, but I just never like imposing on anyone. I enjoyed Sam's company on liberty, but I knew he was planning on getting married. My plans were very different from his. Besides, three was always a crowd. Sam sort of understood how I felt but he said somehow things would be different this weekend. Like he knew how I felt all along. Sam wanted me to meet this girl. He told me a hell of a lot about her, seeing how she lived next door to his girl's house. After describing the package, Sam didn't have to twist my arm any more. We went, and I met her.

Her name was Angie Duras; she had brown eyes and long brown hair. She was very, very nice.

The next day I was still at Sam's house. We took some pictures, and then I spent some more time with Angie.

17

Later that night Angie talked her father into driving Sam and me back to the base. The girls rode back with us, and it gave us another hour to be together. It was tough holding onto the last few minutes, but when the weekend was over it was the best liberty so far.

It was Monday again, and our sixth day of training; we were getting closer to leaving. Each training day meant more and more to us. The days went by, and the training kept getting harder, but it still meant quite a bit to us. We had still more training out in the field and also in squad tactics.

On Thursday we were out all night sleeping in foxholes and going out on patrols. It was really cold. At the break of day we assaulted a hill. The squad also had a summary on what we did through the morning. Our squad was in the field most of Friday and, toward evening, we were told to turn in our rifles once we got back to the area. They told us we wouldn't be needing them any longer for our training. At least that was a few pounds we didn't have to carry any longer.

On Saturday, February 4, I took off for Monterey, California to see my brother. I didn't know how many more weekends I would have, and I just had to see some part of my family. I really liked being with Angie, but she wasn't my wife, and Chuck was my brother! It had been more than a year since I last saw Chuck, and it was really good to see him. He was in army intelligence and Uncle Sam was getting ready to send him out, possibly to Saigon, in April. The odds of him not going were against him. Uncle Sam also had more definite plans for me. I knew where I was going; I just didn't know when. What Uncle Sam was faced with were two brothers that couldn't fight his war at the same time.

After Chuck and I got the military talk out of the way, we went swimming. Later on we played badminton, and at night Chuck, Sue, and myself visited another couple in their apartment.

We spent a nice quiet evening. I tried to hide the nervous feeling I had, but Chuck had no problem noticing it.

In the morning, I was still with my brother. We did some more swimming and we played more badminton, just to keep my mind off leaving. I took some pictures of my brother and his wife and then packed the camera away. Chuck drove me to the airport and I caught the 5:45 P.M. flight back to Los Angeles. When I was on the plane, I couldn't help wondering if I would ever see my folks or sisters or brothers ever again. Only God knew that! From here on out, he's the only one that could really take care of me.

On Monday, we didn't do much at all. The squad had classes almost all day. One of the sergeants gave us a lecture on escape and evasion. At night we saw a movie on prisoners of war. If nothing else, that got us thinking again.

Today was T-12, our twelfth day of training. This was the day we had our escape and evasion. It took all day, and part of Wednesday morning. It sure was a bitch!

It all started when they drove us by truck out in the fields. The sergeant told us to get out and form two single lines, one on each side of the road. We were to walk along the road at about three yards between each other. The other outfit involved in this was the aggressor. We were to escape at any time from this point on. If we made it back to the trucks without being caught, the escape was successful. A few marines dove off the side of the road into shrubbery while we were rounding the bend. Most of us were too damn curious as to what this was all about, so we didn't try to escape until we got to where we were going. As we kept walking, the aggressors set up two checkpoints for us to get back to after the escape. We were taken to a large barbed wire circular compound. We were given rice and cups of water. This was all we were going to get until we got back to our training area, which was to be the next morning. After the sergeant had herded us into the compound, they let four marines escape at a time—each group escaping ten minutes apart. By this time, it was almost dark, and this made it even harder to find the checkpoints. When it was our turn to leave the compound, I found myself with Sacorsky and two other marines, strangers. Since the roads were covered with aggressors, we had to find another way to the checkpoints. Everything we had tried to memorize in the daytime didn't help us now. This explained why we were not blindfolded. Luckily there was almost a full moon, and the only thing that stood out at night were the massive power lines. The four of us knew that these power lines ran pretty close to the road. It was our decision to head for the closest power line and follow it to the road.

We were bound to see the fire at one of the checkpoints. The furthest thing from my mind was that this escape and evasion might cost me my life. Well, believe me, it almost did!

After two or three hours of walking in the dark, we were pretty damn cold, hungry, and cut up from the tall grass and bushes. And on top of everything else, it started to rain. We kept following the power lines, sometimes going up on high ground and then leveling off again. We had no idea by this time how far up we had been going from the road.

When we spotted the fire, we were really shocked to know that now we had to go down quite a ways to get to the road. Sacorsky started his way down through the bushes. I was second, followed by Joe and Roger. We went down along some of the ridges of the wide mountains. As we were coming around one of the ridges, I lost my footing and started sliding down on my belly. I was scared out of my ass and started yelling as I was falling. My hands were trying to grab onto anything. I thought I was a goner. When I hit the edge of the mountain my belt buckle got hung up, and my left hand grabbed a stationary rock. My right hand was still grabbing dirt. Sacorsky heard my yelling and started down after me. I told him no, it was too steep. Sacorsky then took off his blanket roll and lay on his stomach. Roger and Joe then grabbed his ankles and slid him down. He extended his blanket roll and told me to grab onto it. I reached for it with my right hand and then grabbed it with my left. Boy, was I scared! It took the help of all three marines to pull me up. It was the closest I had ever come to being killed. Thanks, Lord; I needed you then!

When we got to the checkpoint, I was still pretty shaken up. I also couldn't thank the fellows enough for what they did. They told me to forget it; it could have happened to any one of us. The fact that it didn't happen to them kept me from sleeping. After some of the marines had a few hours sleep, we were taken back to Mainside.

The next morning we took some more shots and then turned in our field jackets, along with the rest of our 782 gear. It was now our last training day, and all that was scheduled was a combat-ready physical test. This was just to keep us in shape, and to see how well we'd come in our training. It was an easy day, for a change. After the physical test, they told us to sit down and be quiet. We were told that when liberty call goes in the morning, we should make it a good one. It was brought to our attention that on Wednesday, we would be leaving for Okinawa. They didn't know if we would get liberty or not. It was that close; in no time at all I would be in Vietnam.

21

We were told that the platoon looked good, real good, and that if you got to go to Vietnam, it's best you go well trained. The platoon commander told us that a lot of us fellows would be split up to fill the battalions that had lost men in combat. He said good luck, and told us to keep out heads low. After the little speech, the marines went back to the area and sat around the rest of the day.

It was the next morning, and I took off on liberty with Rich and Ed to find a motel. If I had a choice, my plans would have been to stay with Angie, but I'm sure her parents had different plans. I was invited over at night, but I left at a decent time. Her parents told me to come back in the morning, and I told them I would. Angie's parents liked me, but they knew it wasn't good for their daughter to care for a guy who was leaving for Vietnam. They read the paper every morning, so there was really nothing I could say. When I got back to the motel, Rich and Ed were still out on the town. It wasn't hard for these guys to find something to do.

I finished up my last day of liberty with Angie. It was tough telling her that I wouldn't be seeing her for thirteen months, but I said I would come back before I headed for Illinois. I gave her a Marine Corps ring that I found on base, and told her to keep it for me. Not to wear it, just keep it. It wasn't fair to keep her from going out with anyone else. I told her to remember me but to give herself a chance to find someone that knows what he wants.

Chapter IV

The date was February 13, a Monday. Our training was over, at least in the United States, and we didn't know what was ahead of us.

The platoon had a junk-on-the-bunk inspection. This is when each marine puts military articles on his bunk, in a certain fashion.

When the inspection was over, we packed up our seabags and filled out tags for them. All the marines were really nervous by now. Waiting was the hardest part to get through. In the morning we had our seabags weighed, and then we mostly sat around thinking about the plane ride. There would be a lot of marines flying out tomorrow, including two mortar platoons. Sam and I hoped that we wouldn't get split up, but we didn't know what the odds were of staying together, either.

It was Wednesday now, and the trucks were waiting to take us to the airport. We left by Continental Airlines from El Tora Air Base. We were going to make one stop in Hawaii and then proceed straight on to Okinawa.

On Thursday we were still in the air, and the plane ride was pretty comfortable. We only stayed a half hour in Hawaii while the plane was being serviced. It was long enough for some of the marines to get drunk and tell the waitress or some female tourist that they were in love with them. It didn't matter much, because we arrived in Okinawa early in the morning. They had hot chow waiting for us, and then we were marched over to get our seabags inspected. This was a long process, but well worth the wait. We were given liberty, and it shook the hell out of us. We heard a lot about the Okinawa women, and now we could find out for ourselves how true it really was.

Believe me... it was true what other marines said about Okinawa, and more!

When reveille went at 0530, most of us were still in dreamland. It didn't take long before the sergeants had us sitting in some bleachers, while they passed out handbooks. The handbooks were about the jungle and survival. From this book and from another phase of training we were going to learn the following:

Characteristics of the jungle: jungle hints, health and sanitation, jungle animal life, jungle operations, trapping hints, cooking wild food, and treatment of heat casualties. We were told that the marines' approach to the jungle must be positive. The advantages of conditions found must be explored to the utmost. To do this the marine must know the jungle. This phase of training presents a few methods that marines may employ to effectively cope with the jungle's obstacles while using the helpful aspects of the jungle. Opportunities for the exercise of individual initiative and ingenuity in improvising helpful materials and for improving the jungle living conditions are limitless. Marines can, and must make the jungle work for them.

The instructors went on with a rather lengthy discussion about what our goals are and a little past history of what has been happening so far.

I quote them here: "Our goal is peace in South Asia. The United States has provided economic, technical, and military assistance to Vietnam since 1950. The purpose was to assist the government in developing and maintaining a stable state, capable of resisting attempted aggression or subversion through military means.

"French military forces were defeated in 1954 at Dien Bien Phu, ending the war in Indochina. The Geneva agreements signed by representatives of France and the communist Viet Minh established a truce line dividing Vietnam at the seventeenth parallel and called an end to further aggressive policies from the communists.

"Ho Chi Minh, the communist leader of North Vietnam, assumed South Vietnam would economically and politically collapse and fall under domination from Hanoi.

"By 1955 South Vietnam had gained independence from France and established itself as a free republic.

"In 1961, United States Marine and Army advisors were placed at the battalion level of Vietnamese military units and allowed to accompany them on operations. This greatly increased the advisor's usefulness as they developed techniques and pointed out shortcomings. At the same time, the Marine Corps sent Helicopter Task Element 79.3.3.6 into Vietnam to assist the Vietnamese in their fight against communist insurgents.

"South Vietnam's struggle against the Vietcong was interrupted in 1963 by internal crises arising from disputes between the government and the Buddhists, resulting in a loss of confidence in President Dien by his people.

"The coup occurred within three months, damaging the government's administration. The Vietcong exploited these disruptions by stepping up the attacks with waves of killings and terrorists' acts. With continued United States assistance, the machinery of government moved swiftly to recover its losses.

"On August 2, 1964, three North Vietnamese PT boats fired torpedoes and shells at the destroyer USS *Maddox* on the high seas in the Gulf of Tonkin. Two days later this act was repeated in the same international waters. Response by the United States was swift, as air units struck at bases and other facilities in North Vietnam which supported the attacking boats.

"As a result of the ever-growing threat of communist

25

aggression, the Vietnamese government asked the United States for support and requested combat troops. On March 8, 1965, elements of the Ninth Marine Expeditionary Brigade stormed ashore at Da Nang, Vietnam. On May 8, 1965 this striking force was redesignated the Third Marine Amphibious Force which included some 35,000 marines from the First Marine Division, the Third Marine Division, First Marine Air Wing, and Third Marine Air Wing."

The instructors did say most of us would be going with the First Marine Division or the Third Marine Division. This is where we would be needed the most. These marine forces were now supporting the northern providences of South Vietnam, which included Da Nang, Chu Lai, and Hue.

Before we were told to get off the bleachers, the instructor once again said that we are there in Vietnam because we were asked to help fight against communist aggression. Most of all, marines must remember that their goal in Southeast Asia is to bring about settled conditions that allow the people to form a government of their choosing. When the discussion was finally over, I just couldn't help wondering if Charlie knew why we were there. I guess I would find out soon enough!

The word Charlie was used by many marines as an expression for the word Cong, like in Vietcong.

The weeks passed and we learned our jungle warfare training well. The training was the final touch every marine needed to give him an edge in the paradise fit only for a Cong. The men in the platoon got to know the word survival so well that each letter reminded them of a phrase to keep in mind. The letters of the word are as follows: size up the situation; undue haste makes waste; remember where you are; vanquish fear and panic; improvise; value living; act like the natives; learn basic skills.

All this made sense to us, and we knew that by remembering this word, along with the help of God, some of us marines would make it back.

We left on a Saturday, once again on Continental Airlines. It was very hard to believe that by nightfall, we would be landing in Da Nang, Vietnam. Da Nang was like a rear area, if there was ever such a thing, in Vietnam. There were so many troops that the chances of being overcome were slim. Marines who had to be taken out of the action were sent there. Right now we were thankful that we were not going to be dropped off right in the middle of the action; this kind of stuff would probably come later. When we arrived at Da Nang, we were just as scared and as nervous as we were a few months ago, standing on the yellow footprints at boot camp. It was late, so the officer in charge made us grab a cot, and then we slept all night outside, under some kind of pavillion.

The next morning, bright and early, they started kicking the cots to get us up. One damn good thing about today was that no one was blowing any bugle. How about that? No damn reveille! We were told to fold the cots and sit by our seabags. Our names were being called off left and right, and we saw all our buddies being split up. It didn't look good at all for Sam and me. Sam's name was called first, and he was assigned to the First Marine Division. I didn't know it then, but that was the last time I was to see Sam until my tour in Vietnam was over. We went through all this training together, just so we could get split up as replacements. What a raw deal that was! I was finally called along with five other marines to be assigned to the Fourth Marines, Third Marine Division. When they called out Private Bruce Largo, I couldn't believe it. It was the same big happy thug I met in boot camp on graduation day. It was like it was meant to be. I lost one friend and gained another the very same day. I didn't know him very well yet, but I was going to. The other four marines were Privates Tylor, Davis, Fregon, and Wison.

I knew Wison from our training at the mortar school but never really got tight with him. The six of us were going to be in the same mortar platoon but assigned to different sections. We were taken in a truck to another part of Da Nang where we were to catch the marine transport and supply plane to Dong Ha. Now all that any of us six knew about Dong Ha was that it was further north. In other words, it was closer to Charlie than we really wanted to be. We arrived in Dong Ha, which was quite a place. Not as big as Da Nang, but it still stretched for miles. We were taken to a tent and were told to get some sleep.

The six of us stuck pretty close together, because none of us knew what was happening. The next morning we were given our 782 gear. This gear was to be ours for the next twelve months, hopefully no longer, and hopefully we were to turn it in ourselves.

After our gear was put away back in the tent, some of the fellows wanted to go check out the rest of Dong Ha. I was content where I was, so I decided to stay and write a few letters. I guess Bruce felt the same way because he didn't go either. Bruce and I had a lot in common. We both were single, and we both had good families back home that really cared for us. As in my case, the Army had been wanting to draft him too. We both had a good life back home but had both been getting a little bored.

The one extra thing Bruce had was a lovely girl back home that he thought several times about marrying.

When my letters were written, I lay back on the cot and thought about my family and all the girls that wrote to me, and then off to sleep I went.

The next day, we were indoctrinated by the colonel, and then we had a lecture on the M-16 rifle. I wrote as many letters as I could whenever I could, and I also sat around dreaming whenever I could. Later in the day I took a ride on a mule to pick up beer rations. A mule is like a jeep, except it has a flat bottom for sitting. Our beer ration was two cans, whenever we could get it. Nothing like writing letters while you're drinking two cans of warm beer.

When it came to mail, I was as lucky as a marine could get. I used to have to write letters every chance I could, just to answer all my mail. I started getting more mail than the rest of the marines I was with and kept that trend going throughout my term in Vietnam.

In the morning we were assigned sections and met the platoon commander and the four section leaders. We were given a little refresher course on how things were going to operate over here and on what we would be working with.

The lieutenant called everyone out of his tent for a brief introduction. He said, "Men, the new six replacements bring our platoon to ninety-four enlisted men with two officers. The new men heard this before, but I'd like them to hear it again. This platoon is made up of four firing sections. Each section has two gun squads. It is to provide close and continuous fire support to the rifle companies. I am responsible for the overall operation of the company. The assistant platoon commander will receive his assignments from me. Our platoon sergeant is the gunner sergeant. He is referred to as operation chief, and he assists both of us.

"Our ammo NCO is Sergeant Tammes. His job is to get all the supplies. He must know where the ammo and all supply points are. This platoon has two radio operators,

29

and each section has a wireman. The wiremen work with radios and telephones. Our platoon also has a messenger-driver.

"The six new men will start off as ammo carriers. You will be carrying the aiming stakes or the base plate. The base plate weighs forty-seven pounds, but it comes apart. The outer ring weighs twenty-three pounds, and the inner ring weighs twenty-four pounds. As men rotate back to the States, or for some other reasons, you men will move up to assistant gunners and gunners, maybe even squad leaders, before your time is completed." The six of us knew what he meant when he said "or for some other reasons" and we didn't like that part at all.

The platoon commander continued, "The barrel of the mortar is fifty-one inches long and weighs twenty-eight pounds. The bipods weigh forty pounds and are carried by the gunner.

"The sight of the mortar weighs three pounds and is carried by the squad leader. The mortar weighs 115 pounds complete. The lowest elevation is 700 mills and the highest is 1500 mills. The maximum range is 4,453 meters. The minimum range is fifty meters."

When the introduction was over, we filled the gun pits with ammo, and then we were told that we were moving out in the morning. The six of us went back to the tents to pack and get squared away. Our seabags stayed in Dong Ha in the storage area. From here on out, we take just what we need in the field.

In the morning, some of the marines in the platoon won't be going with us. These lucky fellows are the short-timers. Any marines with less than thirty days left in Vietnam are usually left in Dong Ha until their flight date back to the States.

Chapter V

It was Saturday when the first section moved out for the bridge near Cam Lo. It was about twenty-five miles away, so the trucks took us. Bruce and I were lucky enough to be assigned to the same section and the same gun. We never worried about who carried what, or why; all we wanted to do was go home the same time. As far as seniority goes, we did most of the work together. Davis, Tylor, Wison, and Fregon were now in different sections, but not too far away. If the platoon ever moved out in force, we were sure to see them again.

My first working party in Vietnam came on Sunday. The section leader came into the tent and told me to go string some barbed wire. Bruce was right there on his cot and asked if the working party could use one more guy. The corporal said, "Sure, if you really want to."

Bruce smiled and said, "Why not? I won't be going anywhere for awhile."

Toward evening the section had to pair off to stand lines. It was the first time Bruce and I stood lines in Vietnam. It rained all night.

The next day we slept late, and when we got up it was still raining. I wrote some letters and stood watch in the Fire Direction Center. When I got off watch, I associated with some of the Vietnamese children and their families. All the time, my eye was on a cute little girl everyone called Angel.

Things were pretty quiet around the bridge area, and that is how I got stuck digging a six-foot by six-foot hole for trash. I wasn't alone, and it really wasn't all my fault. It all happened when I was picked to stand lines with Carl Wesson. Carl had been in Vietnam about nine months now, and he was a real salty character. We stood our watch all night, and just before the break of day, Carl said, "Let's go back to the tent. Things are quiet now, and the other watch will be along in ten minutes." I knew better than to leave my post unless properly relieved, but like a dummy I followed Carl back.

It was just my luck that the section leader was checking the post. Better him than the officer in charge, but needless to say, we still had to dig the hole. It took nearly all day, and I learned my lesson well. At night, I was back out on lines with Bruce, hearing him all night telling me I was a dummy.

It was now March 1; time was moving slowly. I went swimming in the river for a while, and then mail call went. I only received a couple of letters, one from my parents and one from Jim. Jim was a buddy of mine from back on the block; he was now serving in the Air Force and always rubbed it in about how good he had it. I believed him, because I saw how the Air Force lived in Da Nang.

Standing lines by the bridge was a regular thing. We didn't know what the Vietcong would do, if they wanted this bridge badly enough. We were allowed to swim in the daytime, as long as another marine was watching the post. We tried to stay busy, so the time wouldn't drag by. One day I pitched in to help some of the other fellows rebuild the pier.

It was time for us to get paid. They cleared the books on me, and I got a whole $98.00. That night I played cards, and sure enough, I lost twenty-three dollars of it. I sent most of my money home, except for a little mad money. Over here, money didn't mean a thing to us.

Today we got ahold of a lot of beer. I never asked where it came from, but it was much more than our normal beer ration. The beer was warm, of course, but it was the first time we had any beer since we left Dong Ha. I received nine letters the same day. That night I got too drunk to stand lines. I didn't even finish reading my mail. Bruce took my watch, and I was thankful for that. He knew I'd do it for him, if he should ever tie one on.

In the morning, I really had a bad hangover, but I went on lines anyway. I also had two hours of FDC watch. It rained all day again. The weather was really shitty, but it probably would get worse. This time of the year is considered the tail end of the monsoon season.

It was still raining today, and most of the section was inside the tent. Up to now, we didn't have any major fire missions, but then some really bad shit happened. Corporal Wade was in the Fire Direction Center when he got the message. He came running out yelling, "Fire mission, fire mission. Get on the guns." We all scrambled for the guns and waited for the order to fire, but we never got the word. Ninth Marines were caught in an ambush, and the Vietcong were too damn far away for our mortars. By the time the Ninth Marines got support, the Vietcong had started to pull back. The Ninth Marines did the same, because they really took a beating. The wounded had to walk, if it was possible. They pulled back to where we were, and what a sickening sight and smell that was. They lost nine men from their 81 Mortar Platoon alone. We had to carry the dead bodies off the tanks, and some of the bodies were not in one piece. The heat from the tanks made the smell unbearable, and I puked more than once. Please Lord, don't let this happen to me! Nick in our platoon lost his good buddy, and we knew what he was going through. We prayed for ourselves that night, and for our buddies. Why does this really have to be?

33

In the morning we got the word that we would be heading back to Dong Ha sometime that day. It didn't matter whether we were leaving or not, because Bruce and I went on another working party to string some more barbed wire. Some other outfit will just take over and do the same routine that we went through.

As soon as the working party was secured, we were ordered to pack up. The trucks were already waiting to take us to Dong Ha. The mortar platoon had not been there long when we found out that we had a big operation planned for tomorrow.

I guess we'll be going after those bastards that attacked the Ninth Marines. After what the Vietcong did to those men, we certainly wanted to get them. I just couldn't help thinking to myself, and almost crying inside, "Ma, Da, I'm really scared. Whatever happens, please take care of yourselves."

Chapter VI

It was March 8 now, and it was also my first operation in Vietnam. We started out early in the morning, and I'll be damned if it didn't start to rain. We humped our mortars to a place where there was nothing but sand. While we were digging in, Charlie let us have a few bursts of small-arms fire. I hit the sand and lay still; I was so damn numb that I could have pissed in my pants and wouldn't have known it until Bruce razzed me about it. As far as I could tell, no one was hit. I remembered what some instructor said back in training. The instructor told us that the first time he was in a fire fight, he stuck close to a gunnery sergeant that had been around for years. He figured if anyone knew the way out, the gunny did. I had my eye on Corporal Wade, and if we went after Charlie, I was sticking with him.

The next order the mortar squad got was to set the guns up and stand by. The rifle companies took off after Charlie and captured three prisoners. It was only the first day, so that was a good start for a successful operation.

The 81 Mortar Platoon wasn't needed today, so we saved our energy.

On the second day of operation we walked 14,000 meters, or, as I said before, humped. About 1,000 meters equals a mile; we walked fourteen miles. We had our guns set up on some mountain. Bruce and I were sore from carrying the aiming stakes and the outer ring of the base-plate. We were both ammo humpers, so we switched off. When we had some time, Bruce and I thought a lot about places we would rather be than on this operation. They didn't even tell us the name of this one yet.

When the helicopters, or choppers, as we called them, came in with supplies, four men from the mortar platoon alone went back because of sore feet.

The next day we pushed on and this time, we were sniped at. We were ordered to set our guns up in the mountains again, and since the mortarmen were not needed any more, the rifle companies took care of the snipers.

It was now the fourth day of operation. We humped 22,000 meters. We were really pushing the Cong back north, but it was tough on some of the marines' feet. The mortar platoon lost five more men: four of them had bad blisters on their feet, and the other marine split his knee open on a rock while crossing a stream. Once the blisters come, you can't take care of them when you continue to have wet feet. When our socks got muddy or ripped, we threw them away and put dry ones on. The trouble was, we couldn't keep them dry going through rice paddies.

We humped some more the next day, and by this time Bruce and I were barely holding up. We weren't as bad as the marines that went back, but at this pace, it was only a matter of time.

The colonel knew everyone's feet were giving out; he also knew tired marines were not as good when they met the enemy.

It was decided that we stay in the same area one more day, but we had to set up a perimeter and nightwatch. Kinly and I took our turn at standing lines.

The Vietcong had been running from us the whole operation; they would only keep a handful at a time back to slow us down with snipers. We pushed on toward transportation, but with more small-arms fire, we couldn't make it just yet. The mortar platoon stayed in the lowlands until morning.

The next day we headed for the road and again were slowed down by sniper fire. However, we did make it, and the trucks picked us up and brought us back to Dong Ha.

After some rest, our section was told that we were going back to guard the bridge. I said to myself, *as soon as I get back, I'm diving into the river and taking a nude bath. I'm also going to catch up on writing some letters.*

It is now March 16 and our section is back guarding the bridge. I already have had my nude bath, and now I'm about to shave off the fuzz on my face. It's been over a month since I shaved.

Bruce and I got off a few quick letters to home, and it was hard not to feel depressed and lonely. We wrote how we felt, so the letters were not very cheerful. Later on during the day, Bruce and I went down and talked with Angel, the little Vietnamese girl. She was glad to see us, and she knew we had our laundry for her. For the most part, it was very hard to trust the Vietnamese people.

Today in the tent, there was talk of another operation, because the bad news was that another element of the Ninth Marines was wiped out. If there ever was a bad luck outfit, Ninth Marines was it. Most of the fellows were guessing that we would be going back into the fields. I didn't want to think about that, so I began drinking my beer ration and Bruce's too. I could always count on Bruce's ration, because he didn't like drinking warm beer. It was nice when we got drunk on warm beer; we didn't have to think about being over here.

I woke up early, because I wanted to catch up with answering all my mail. The mortarmen have been standing lines every night, but there has been talk of the rifle companies doing more of the watching. The colonel wants us working with the guns more, so we don't get stale. We run practice missions every day, but it's never the same as when it really counts. We have a tendancy to get lazy.

On this particular day, I didn't have any FDC watch, and I was glad. There was no rain today, and boy, was it hot. I went back to the tent and Bruce was writing a few letters while some of the other fellows were listening to the music from their record player. Since Bruce was busy, I went to my cot for some relaxation. I never got to relax because of Private Mesley. This guy wasn't too well liked by anyone, but for some reason the situation was worse between Bruce and Mesley. Mesley had been giving Bruce a hard time lately, really rubbing him the wrong way. I guess Bruce took this shit long enough and then exploded. It all happened so fast that I couldn't help getting involved.

Mesley came in from taking his watch, and I guess he was in a bad mood. He started messing Bruce's hair up and fooling with Bruce's writing material. Bruce grabbed his arm and shoved him back towards the opening of the tent. Mesley hated Bruce even more for this, and pulled out a knife. I jumped up and kicked the knife out of Mesley's hand, and then gave him a chop across the ribs. By this time, Bruce pulled me out of the way and took over. Mesley never got to lay a hand on Bruce. He started to throw his fist, but Bruce caught him in the face first. Bruce then gave him a forearm to his head twice. Mesley went down, and after a couple of kicks from Bruce, the fight was broken up. Bruce went back and finished his letter, and I had a warm beer.

In the morning, Bruce and I were told to go on a working party to string cans with buckshot in them. Then we tied the cans to the barbed wire. At night we stood lines together, and Bruce talked about the girl he cared for back home. He told me I'm welcome to come home with him, when we get back. I said sure, providing your girl will fix me up with someone.

It is March 20, and so far things haven't changed much. If the war doesn't get any worse for this section, I won't register any complaints. Most of the guys hardly did anything today. We went swimming again, as well as took our baths.

I received my first package from my parents.

Some of the guys couldn't help getting bored, and others joked around or did anything that would make them happy. On an operation it was just the opposite. We never got bored, and most of the time we were too busy, and too scared, to be happy.

We never knew when Charlie would open up on us from an ambush. We had to sweat it out. It seemed like we were always sweating it out over here.

There had been talk that we might be going back to Okinawa for replacements. There were a lot of men getting ready to go back to the States, which meant more new faces in the section and squads. The faces here were always changing, like in many other squads. We were like a temporary family.

The section leader came up to the tent and told us to get our 782 gear cleaned. The lieutenant wanted to inspect our gear and our rifles before anyone hit the sack for the night. This was a good sign, so the fellows started thinking of Okinawa again. Okinawa meant a lot of things to us. We knew we could sleep as much as we wanted again. We could have hot chow and clean white sheets everyday. At night when it got cold, we could have blankets. In the daytime we could go outside of the squad bay, take off our boots and socks and wiggle our toes in the fresh air. If it rained, we could go inside and keep dry. We could take hot showers every day, and the fellows could stand in them for hours. It meant good liberty, a lot of cold beer, and plenty of women. Not necessarily in that order!

Even though we were to get up at 0600 the next morning, I kept writing letters. I wanted to get caught up on my mail. So far I've answered every letter, and I hope I can always do this. If there's any one thing that will keep me going, it is my mail. I write more letters than any marine in the section, maybe even the platoon, but I'm proud to say that I receive more mail than anyone else.

The section had everything looking good, and we were really anxious about getting on that ship and getting out of this country. Everything went on as usual, because no word came down to us.

Bruce and I were still standing lines every night and still taking baths in the river.

Our section acquired a machine gun today, and because Bruce and I had been in Vietnam the least amount of time, we were told to clean it.

Every day one or two marines from our section would go back and get their seabags from Dong Ha. They would bring them back to the bridge and get everything squared away.

It was only a matter of time before we would head for the ship. All the guys were now talking about Okinawa. Some would leave for the States when they got there. Their time in Vietnam was over.

Bruce and I were on lines, and I guess Bruce remembered what day it was, because he looked at me and said, "Happy Easter, Vichelli."

"Well, I'll be—thanks Bruce!"

All the men in the section wanted to be home so much.

Chapter VII

I went down in the morning and gave Angel my laundry, and then most of the guys went for a swim.

I wasn't feeling too good, so I went back to the tent and hit the sack early. When I woke up, I was burning with a temperature. I also was sick to my stomach. Bruce was like a big ugly nurse over me. It was good having him around though. He did what he could for me, making sure I took Anacin and later Bayer aspirin. Nothing seemed to help. I got some hot soup down me and then bundled up, hoping I could break the fever. I couldn't help hearing Wade tell the rest of the guys that we're going on a small operation in the morning. He told Bruce that if I still had a fever, I would be sent back to Dong Ha.

I wanted to stay with Bruce and the rest of the section so much that I asked the Lord to take care of me.

The fever did break, but I was still very weak. We left straight from the bridge and started walking. We humped a little over 4,000 meters, and there was no sign of any Vietcong. Bruce stayed close, in case I had any trouble.

The second day of operation we humped about 6,000 meters. We were positive that we were in the same area as on the last operation. Still no contact with the Vietcong.

It was now April 1, and we started heading back toward the bridge. The forward observer spotted some Vietcong near the village, so we stayed another night and sent patrols out.

On the fourth day of operation, we swept two villages and moved on to Highway 101.

The prisoners we caught were sent to Dong Ha, and our section was brought back to the bridge by trucks.

The order came through for our platoon to get ready to catch the ship in Dong Ha.

We were to get our gear cleaned up again, and we were to wait in Dong Ha until the ship was ready to leave.

Once we got to Dong Ha, we got paid. Also, the whole platoon had to get haircuts, except the few marines that had their heads shaved; they wouldn't have to get a haircut this time.

I wrote some letters, and sent home a two-hundred–dollar check. That was better than blowing all the money in Okinawa.

Bruce and I had never been on a ship before, and we thought about it most of the night.

To keep our minds off it, we got into a card game. Bruce didn't do too badly, and I won forty-five dollars.

We hit the sack finally, and had no problem sleeping. On April 5, we left for the ship. When we got there, we had to go up the nets. It was the first time we had done this since our training. The whole platoon went up without any trouble.

The navy wanted at least one man from each section aboard the ship for mess duty. It was a toss-up between Bruce and myself again. I told Bruce I would do it. Bruce has been a hell of a guy from the start, and I figured I could even the score.

The rest of the marines in the platoon had to start getting ready for an inspection.

I worked all morning on mess duty, and then I was given a few hours break. I went back to the compartment and lay in the rack.

The next day was more of the same, except I wrote some letters. After evening mess was over, Bruce and I saw the movie *Thunder Island*.

Today was our fifth day on the ship. I wrote some more letters when I got the chance and saw as many movies as I could. The movie I saw tonight was called *Seven Faces of Dr. Lau.*

It was April 10 now, and I was still on mess duty. In the afternoon I went on deck and took some pictures. The word was passed that we would be pulling into Okinawa tomorrow.

I reported to mess duty as usual, but I was only there for a little while. We docked in Okinawa early, so the mess chief told me to go back to my section.

When all the marines, as well as our trucks and jeeps, were off the ship, we were taken to Camp Hansen. We were assigned squad bays and lockers and began unpacking our gear.

I was almost unpacked when I heard my name being mentioned. It was a guy looking for Vichelli. I looked down towards the end of the squad bay, and I couldn't believe my eyes. It was Al Meed. We threw our arms around each other, and I was never so glad to see anyone. The last time I saw Al was back home, in May of 1966, almost a year ago now.

I finished throwing my gear in the locker and asked the section leader if I could take off for a few hours. I asked Bruce to come along, but he said he would catch up to us at the club.

Al and I had so much to talk about but didn't have nearly enough time. His outfit was leaving in the morning to go back to Vietnam. His outfit had been here a month, for the same reasons our outfit was: More training and more replacements. We drank and drank at the club, not wanting to call it a night. I asked how his girl, Mary, was, and he told me that he was planning on getting married.

Al wanted me to do him a special favor. I said, "Sure, Al, anything." He had ordered some suits for when he got

43

home and had them in for tailoring. They weren't ready, so he asked me to get them and send them home to his brother.

His folks had died, and he was staying with his brother and his brother's wife. Al had less than ninety days left in Vietnam. We stayed at the club until we were chased out around 1:00 in the morning. We laughed and joked, and finally we made the move back to the barracks.

Al is a great guy, and I'm praying everything will go well for him when he gets back to Vietnam. The outfit I'm attached with will be going the same place as his outfit, as soon as we're ready.

(I didn't know it then, but that night was to be the last night I was to ever see Al Meed again. When he got back to Vietnam, his outfit pulled a major operation. While the marines were taking a hill, a sniper's bullet found Al. Al Meed's life ended quickly on Saturday, May 20, 1967. I served my complete term in Vietnam, and never was told of Al's death. My mother, for her own special reasons, never wrote me about it. As you will see, it turned out to be to my advantage that I never knew.)

The rumors were now going around that we wouldn't actually start any classes, or any training until Monday. Since it was only Wednesday, it gave us plenty of time to get our gear squared away and to enjoy some more of that Okinawa liberty. We couldn't leave the base until 1800, so I caught up on my letter writing.

I thought about Al Meed a lot, feeling good inside that his term was almost over. I'm also looking forward to when I, too, will only have a short time to go.

When liberty call went, Bruce and I ended up in New Koza and took up where we left off in February. We didn't know each other the first time we came through Okinawa, but being in Vietnam with Bruce for just two months, I'm glad I know him now. We went on liberty almost every night together and were together on working parties during the day. When Friday came, Bruce and I were given our first forty-eight hour pass in our time with the Marine Corps.

The first thing we did was get a room. The room only cost $6.00, but we didn't get to sleep in it until 5:00 in the morning.

We had five hours sleep and woke up with our heads spinning and our bellies aching. Bruce and I wanted to do something different, so we met a cab driver, named Danny, and he took us all around for some fine sight seeing. At night we got drunk again and stayed at the Hotel Lucky.

When we woke up this time, it was 2:00 Sunday afternoon. We spent the rest of the day at the Club Nighter and the Castle Club.

We listened to an all-girl band called the Amazons. It was now April 17, and the classes started over again. We were taught how to use the plotting boards, and had a class on the M-16 rifle. After the class, we were issued our new rifles. We did our usual physical training, before our new platoon commander inspected our lockers. Our shore liberty was secured, so Bruce, Davis, Tylor, and myself went to the base club and then to the bowling alley.

It was the first time I bowled in just under a year. It was different from when I bowled as a civilian. When I was home, it meant so much to me, and now I have too many other things on my mind to really enjoy the sport.

Every day was routine now, more classes, more training, although the nights were very different. Anything went once we were off the base, as long as we were careful.

It wasn't unusual to be lonely, and the more girls I

saw, the more I wanted to get to know them. One of the girls I met was Nakate; among everything else, she was a good dancer.

I really enjoyed being with her, because it sure beat slopping down beer in the corner by yourself or with another jarhead. I made a date with her for Sunday.

She was the first girl I made a date with since I had been overseas. It was like asking girls back home; the only difference was that I felt I knew the girls a little better back home.

I saw her again the next night, which was Thursday. I played it straight with Nakate, like I would with any girl, thinking about spending a nice quiet Sunday together.

The date was still on, so I asked her where I could meet her. She told me in front of the club at 1:00 P.M.

On Friday morning our platoon went to the rifle range and fired the M-16 rifles. We had to field day the barracks for inspection when we got back, and then most of us hung around. Tomorrow was going to be a busy day.

The first thing in the morning, we took our physical readiness test. Everyone passed, and then we had another inspection. When liberty call finally went, I really didn't feel like going anywhere, probably because I only had enough money to cover a decent date with Nakate.

I hung around the barracks and shot the breeze with Bob and Sergeant Morrisey.

It was now Sunday, and I woke at eleven o'clock after having plenty of sleep. I was really feeling great, singing in the shower.

I got to the club a little before 1:00, but no one was there yet. I waited around until finally a cab pulled up. A girl rolled down the window and asked if my name was Mike. When I nodded my head yes, she told me she was a friend of Nakate.

46

She went on to tell me that Nakate wouldn't be coming, because she was busy at another job. The girl smiled and wanted to know if the cab driver could take me anywhere. I said, "Thanks, but no thanks, I have to think this one out." Then the cab driver took off.

I didn't have to be a general to know what Nakate's other job might be. I was really had and with a smile on top of that.

It was the first time something like that ever happened to me, and I was damn sure going to try to make it my last time. All along I was playing it straight with her, while she was willing to be anybody's girl, for a price.

The lesson was well learned, and I had a feeling I was going to learn a lot more before I got back to the States.

On Monday, April 24, it seemed to a lot of us that the training had been stepped up. We already felt that we wouldn't be in Okinawa as long as we thought. Our platoon was taken to a place called Jungle Lane.

Here we climbed ropes, went through muddy rivers and over some mountains. The damn thing lasted all day.

In the morning I was picked along with Bruce for a working party. All we did was sand and paint some boards, and then we policed the area until dark.

The next day consisted of classes and demonstrations on mines and demolitions. We learned how to set them and place them in the ground, and also how to disarm them. The classes lasted all day.

On Friday, we had a personal inspection, just before the paymaster arrived. Everybody rushed to get in line, and everybody got paid except me. I was NPD which means *no pay due*. I had thought I was overpaid the last time, but I really didn't care about giving any of it back. Now they caught up with me, and I'll suffer all month for it.

The next day we had another small inspection, this

time by the section leader. Then we had some pictures taken of us as a platoon. They also took pictures of the section and of individuals.

After we got up the next day, Bruce and Kincannon offered to lend me some money. They hated to leave me behind when they decided to go to Kin Village, so I gave in and went with them. We had a great time, and they paid for everything.

In the morning there had been a lot of working parties going on at Motor Transport. The work was enough to tire me out, and being the early part of the week, I didn't go anywhere. In fact, I was in bed before midnight for the first time since we arrived in Okinawa.

On Tuesday, we had gun drill all day. We were told to get a field marching pack ready, because we would soon be in the field.

Early the next day we took off, and we reached a place that nobody knew. We were told to pitch our tents. We no sooner got them up than it started to rain. We didn't fire the mortars, but we did find time to fire our rifles.

We had classes again on the care and cleaning of the M-16. We also had some more inspections, followed by more classes on FDC and the plotting board. The weekend came fast, and we were told that Monday the platoon would be practicing for the field meet.

Most of the guys caught up on some letter writing. I did get into town for a while, and got to meet a buddy from back home. I was at a wedding with him before we left the States. This was the first time I had seen him since.

Before we knew it, another week went by, and all we did was have more working parties and more classes, and have our battalion field meet. I also got to see two movies. One was with Ann Margaret and the other was called, *What Did You Do in the War, Daddy?*

It was Saturday again, the day for our memorial services parade. It lasted all morning. The purpose was to honor the men we lost in Vietnam since January and the men who won purple hearts. When it was over, liberty call went at 1200.

The next day we were told to pack for Vietnam. We also got paid. I received forty-one dollars, and that almost took care of my debts.

Our liberty was secured, but after my packing was complete, I was talked into going to the village. I tried over and over to get Bruce to go, and finally the four of us were on our way for another look at Kin Village.

It was the first time any of us ever did something like this. We went to the back of the base, over a wall, and through a hole in the fence. The agreement we made was to meet at the Mikado Restaurant at 0500 and then head back to base while it was still dark. Red and Bruce had some places they wanted to check out, so Bob and I went for a few beers. Before we got wasted on beer, we met some very interesting girls, keeping in mind how much time we had for them. We finally managed to break away and get to the restaurant at 0445. Bob and I waited until 0515, and then time was running out for us. We had to be back before it became light, or we would surely be caught. There were over two miles of cathouses, and we didn't even know where to begin looking.

We got back into the base the same way, always hoping that somehow Red and Bruce were not far behind us. We made it out of our clothes and into the racks and slept for an hour before reveille went at 0700.

When we jumped out of the racks, we asked around if anyone saw Bruce or Red. Nobody saw either of them. When we heard this, Bob and I almost got sick to our stomachs. We were aware of what could happen if they

49

missed the platoon movement. It didn't take long at all before the platoon was herded out for roll call like cattle. Our gear was with us, so we were told to get in the trucks as our names were called. When Bruce's name was called, nobody moved. When the sergeant asked if anybody knew where he might be, we came forward and were told to wait in the CO's office.

We spilled the beans about Bruce and Red, and believe me, it was for their benefit. The lieutenant really laid into us, telling us we were foolhearted but lucky marines, lucky to have made it back in time, a lot luckier than Bruce and Red. The convoy left on schedule for the airport, and Bob and I couldn't help thinking about our buddies, still in town someplace. The MPs were already out looking for them.

As the convoy was rolling along, some jarhead yelled out for us to look at this cab barreling down the highway. We only caught a glimpse of what looked like Bruce in the back seat and Red in the front. Bob and I hoped that there would still be time to get them on that plane with us. As it turned out, there was a delay at the airport, and Bruce and Red, still in their civilian clothes, were driven down in a military vehicle. They were pretty shaken up by all this and didn't say too much. When Bruce finally did say something to me, he was really concerned about his military record. He said, "Mike, I really did a dumb thing, and now I'm going to have to pay for it. Charges of AWOL and missing a military movement are being brought against Red and myself, as soon as we get off the operation. Maybe I won't be around after the operation for them to send to jail, or whatever they do to guys over here."

Bruce broke down and didn't talk much more after that, but I did find out a little more. Bruce was going through all this suffering because he overslept with some whore. I didn't know much about Red, or if he had ever been through something like this before, but I did know what made Bruce tick, and this was eating him up inside.

I knew where my place was going to be on the next operation: right beside Bruce. I knew I would help him all I could. My only hope was that it would be enough.

Chapter VIII

The plane landed at Dong Ha, and it was the second time for Bruce and me in three months. The first time we were still green, but now we came back with some bad memories of Vietnam. We pitched shelter halves and dug our holes not far from the air strip. The squad took turns taking gunwatch. It only was for an hour this time, and I had mine in the early evening.

The next day was spent on cleaning our rifles and getting all our gear organized for when we pull out. The operation was close in coming, and everyone was a little jumpy. I managed to get a letter written home before I was picked for a working party to go after some ammo. When we came back with the ammo, the humpers were given three rounds apiece to make up their pack boards. I was also told by the corporal to dig my hole deeper. I thought it was deep enough, but after all, what do I know?

The Vietcong must have known we were coming and wanted us to have a little taste of what we could expect on the operation. As soon as it got dark, they mortared the hell out of us. It was May 17, and it was the first time I had been under mortar fire. It was quite an experience.

I wasn't near my hole when the first round came in, and when the second one hit, I dove on top of two marines already in a hole built comfortably for one. They didn't mind me being on top of them as long as they were able to breath. The thing that worried me was that I couldn't get my ass down far enough. It wasn't the best part of me, but I still didn't want it blown off.

At the break of day we were flown by helicopter into the DMZ. To our knowledge, it was the first time marines made an offensive attack in the DMZ.

It was called Operation Hickory. The first couple of days we didn't move very far. I unloaded helicopters and dug my hole deeper whenever I got the chance. This stuff was still pretty new to me. Up until now, everything was quiet. When we did move on, the platoon humped 250 meters and everybody had to dig in again. Bruce Largo and I were told to stand lines and that we would be relieved in the morning. We did all our talking before it got dark, and I knew that what happened to Bruce in Okinawa was still bothering him. When we were relieved from lines, the corporal told us to go back to the squad and help dig the gunpit.

The squad had been digging for about an hour, and then we got word to pull out closer to North Vietnam. We humped 1,800 meters, and then we set the guns up for a fire mission. It was night, and when the fire mission ended, we were told that we mortared a village in North Vietnam just shortly before a truce went into effect.

We moved on in the morning until we came across some terrain that made for excellent cover against Charlie, the Cong. Trenches were nearby, so the squad took advantage of them and didn't bother digging in this night. Some were big enough for the whole squad to get in.

When it got light, we pushed further on after Charlie, right toward North Vietnam. The Vietcong kept staying ahead of us.

Every chance I got, I worked on the 81 mortar, learning as much as I could. I knew I'd be a gunner someday but never thought that day would come so soon. When we're not practicing on the mortars, we're reading our mail over and over again. On this day I was reading a letter from

Sandy, who was the last girl I was with before I left for this place. It was nice dreaming about her, but sweet dreams don't last long, because as the sergeant walked by he kicked my boots and reminded me that I was standing lines tonight. Every so often, the 81 mortarmen help the grunts stand lines, when the grunts get spread pretty thin around the perimeter. Oh well, so much for Sandy!

It was now the ninth day of operation, and we were near North Vietnam. Our objective was to sweep to the river and then head back in a different direction. I didn't know where we would wind up. The Vietcong had their fun this time, they mortared us before it got dark.

The next day we were resupplied, and mail did come in. I got one post card.

Some more days passed, and our battalion met up with the Second Battalion 26th Marines. The battalions stayed together that night, and both were mortared. Casualties were light.

Our battalion stayed put, giving the men plenty of rest. During the night we fired the mortars to harrass the Vietcong.

When we did pull out, we headed towards the mountains and caught sniper fire most of the way. The grunts took it the worst, but still they kicked some ass.

It was now June 1, the fifteenth day of operation. I managed to write another letter home, and I remember closing it off by saying, "I'm fine, outside of being lonely, homesick, tired, rundown, depressed, and fed up. Don't worry, Ma. Your son, Mike."

The operation went on, and the terrain got rougher. At one point, the underbrush was so thick that it made it almost impossible to hump the mortars through it. They called for helicopters, and we were flown to our next objective.

54

There had been talk of the operation coming to an end, and we were not sure if our mission or purpose was accomplished. We couldn't help wondering if all this was worth it or for that matter if anything we did over here was worth it. Supplies came in again, but this time there was no mail. The morale of the men was really down.

The next day we crossed a river, and luckily it was when the sun seemed the hottest. It gave us a chance to fill our canteens while crossing. For the most part, we were all cool and comfortable, except for Chovene. When Chovene went to drink from his canteen, he damn near swallowed a leech or bloodsucker. It hit his lip and then fell back into the river. On the other side of the river we dug in for the night, and we had hot chow flown in to us. Each marine was also given three cans of beer. It was warm, but believe me, it was good.

Morning came fast, but when we humped to the highway, we saw a welcome sight. There was a whole fleet of trucks waiting to take us to another place.

The word had finally come out; the name of the place was called Camp Carroll. Yes, this operation was finally over, after twenty-two days.

The paymaster came around in the morning and interrupted our working parties. When we were paid, everyone went back to work. Some of the men were cleaning their rifles; others were filling sandbags or loading and dumping trash. During the day, Bruce and I finally got issued our first pair of jungle boots and jungle utilities. Bruce didn't think he would be wearing his very long, once the lieutenant got through with him. The incident in Okinawa still had to be taken care of.

That time finally came, and word was sent down to Bruce that the lieutenant wanted to see him. I wanted to go with Bruce to help however I could, but the sergeant said, "No, just Bruce goes." He was gone for over an hour, and then came back with his head hung low. I couldn't think of how it might be if they transferred him back. Before I could find out anything, Bruce grabbed me and threw me up in the air. I really thought the guy had flipped out. He threw a bear hug on me, and as he put me down gently, he said, "Mike, I've been given another chance. The lieutenant dropped all charges."

That was some happy day, one of so few. Bruce was told that the charges were dropped because his record is clean, he's a good marine, and he had done a fine job on his first operation. I was happy for Bruce. He is a hell of a marine, and he is a hell of a buddy.

For the most part, Camp Carroll had been pretty quiet. The army was here, and one thing for certain, we were able to get plenty of C-rations, but we had to help ourselves to them when it got dark.

We stood lines here every night, and in the day, we ran gun drill and had more working parties. Some were even different, like laying barbed wire. Days passed with no news of any kind of where we might be going, but this place certainly didn't need the army and the marines both here. It wasn't always possible to stand lines with Bruce, because it all depended on whether he was in the area at the time we pulled out for the perimeter. I had been standing lines for sixteen nights with Sal and then the word came down that the mortar platoon was to supply more men to guard the water point. Everyone got shuffled around, and Bruce and I got back together in the same hole. We sure argued a lot and fought about stupid things, but when it came right down to it, we could stand having each other around.

On Monday, July 3, our section was told that Dong Ha and Con Thien were hit with rockets and mortars and under fire from an artillery piece that has a range of twenty-three miles. First Battalion Ninth Marines were there and the talk was that they lost fifty-one men, and another forty-seven were missing under the bunkers and in trenches.

We were issued gas masks because the Vietcong were believed to be using nerve gas, one of the deadly gases.

Since there was a possible attack of ground forces, every hole and bunker had at least three men. It was 100 percent alert, which meant no one sleeps. Santo had been with Bruce and myself all night. Nothing came of the ground attack.

The next day had been a little different; the Vietcong didn't hit us with ground forces, but with 120 mortars. One of the marines from Lima Company caught some shrapnel, but he'll be okay. The round hit near the next trench over, and for Bruce and me, that was close enough.

We've been standing lines for twenty-three days straight now, and everyone is really worn out. There hasn't been much mail coming in, because no one has had the time to write any letters home. The morale is very low, and to make things worse, I received a letter from the folks saying Jayne Mansfield had been killed in a car crash.

The next operation came up fast; we didn't know, as usual, where we would wind up, or when. The name of this was Operation Buffalo. The first night we stayed not far from Camp Carroll. Helicopters brought in food and ammo, but no mail. We dug in and stayed put, and we felt like we were setting an ambush. After a couple of days of this, our platoon was brought to Camp Carroll and told not to unpack anything. It was just for the night. Tomorrow we would know our new destination.

Tomorrow came, and so did the bad news. The place we were headed for would have been our last choice, if we had one. It was Con Thien. A very long ride by trucks. It was still light out when we got there, so we put the guns up first thing and then moved into the bunkers. Bruce and I were scared, but even the fellows that had been over here longer had bad feelings about this place. It was like a nightmare; nothing good comes from it. Many marines were killed here, and we felt that death lingered all around. It even smelled bad!

Bruce and I have been together since our training, and have been with the first section, first gun, since Cam Lo bridge. When Sergeant Meyer took over the section, he told Bruce and me that we would have to get split up on different guns some day, because we couldn't become A-gunners, gunners, or squad leaders at the same time. This made sense, and besides that, we could still stay in the same section. Our time overseas started from February 15, which left us only eight months to go.

The bunkers here are big but need a lot of work. Bruce and I added another rack to ours so that three marines could stay in it. We filled hundreds of sandbags for another ammo bunker and finally put up another wall outside of our door. Before we turned in for the night, I wrote two letters.

I was picked for an early gun watch, so when I was relieved, I grabbed my helmet, filled it with water and began taking a bath. Although water was scarce at this place, the bath was really needed. I no sooner started smelling good again then I was reminded that it was my turn to burn the shitters, one of the choice jobs in Vietnam.

On Monday we had a short inspection of our rifles, and then some of the guys wrote letters. I had received over twenty letters in the last three days and had a lot of catching up to do.

Wednesday came, and the whole platoon was out

policing the area, better known as picking up the papers and garbage. In the afternoon I went to church services, which were held in a big bunker. When mail came in, I received a letter from Bob Tyler. He was a marine that went AWOL in Okinawa. It seemed that Bob fell in love and wanted to marry this girl from the restaurant. No one could talk him out of it, and while he was on liberty one night, he just never came back to the base. That was the last time Bruce or I ever saw him. In his letter, he mentioned that he did get married and was still hiding out. Bob also said that he had done a dumb thing, because now the marriage seemed all bad. Bob was thinking of giving himself up. He ended his letter by saying, "Tell the fellows 'Hi,' and take care of yourselves."

It was now July 22, and the working party that I was on worked like the local garbage men back home. Two men ride in the back of a truck and load trash cans, and then dump them in another spot. I got back to the area late, cleaned up, and read my mail. Another week was over, and the letters that were waiting for me totaled thirty-nine in seven days. Just before we were ready to turn in, Sergeant Meyer came to our bunker and told Bruce that in the morning, he was to go to the second squad as an A-gunner. The time had come for Bruce and me to be split up. I myself would be an A-gunner too, in a couple of days.

We've been here for eleven days now, and Charlie's starting to get restless again. A recon patrol went out this morning and ran into a Vietcong ambush. We lost four men, but the rest of the patrol was reinforced and made it back okay. They spotted the Vietcong building cement bunkers 200 meters from our perimeter. This was about 6:00 A.M.

Toward the afternoon, we caught a little over twenty rounds of mortars, but only one marine was wounded.

It's almost dark now, and it's been a long day. All the days here seem like they're never going to end.

The morning started off hot, and both squads were up early filling sandbags. Bruce and I were both A-gunners now, which meant staying with our squads more. I saw Bruce from time to time because our gun pits were only about twenty-five meters apart. It just wasn't the same as before; I missed talking with him about the things back home. After we had our C-rations for lunch, we ran some gun drill. I was learning the 81 mortar real well, because some day I would be a gunner. The whole squad was in the gun pit. Some of the guys were cleaning their rifles, and Saufo and Travis were stocking some ammo. It was just about dark when the Vietcong let go with what sounded like a rocket. It hit outside the perimeter, so no one moved too much. When the second round came in, it wasn't far from our gun pit, and that's when every marine went for his hole or bunker. The Vietcong were what we call walking the rounds in on us. By the time the third round hit, our whole squad had made it to the bunker. Shit! It was close, too. It had been too damn close. We didn't know exactly where the round hit, but marines were screaming. Sergeant Meyer was yelling, "Fire mission, get on the guns." The squad took off out of the bunker, all except for me. I thought to myself, *screw the fire mission. I have to see how my buddy Bruce is doing.* I ran around the back of the bunker and headed for gun two. Tom had been running to our bunker when I caught him. He was full of blood. He said, "Largo and the rest were hit bad; help Kincannon." I got to the top of the gun pit, and couldn't go any further. My legs froze. I couldn't believe this really happened. Dukol was hit bad, lying in the corner; Chovene was hit bad, and so was Kincannon. I was still on top of the gun pit yelling for Bruce, while

Kincannon kept saying, "I'm sorry, Vichelli, forgive me. I can't find Largo. I don't know where he's at; please forgive me." By this time, I was a basket case. I had flipped out. I wanted to keep yelling until all this was over. The last I remember about the whole bloody night was being dragged off the gun pit.

Bob Saufo was one of the few men that knew I was keeping a diary. He didn't want to write in it, but he did take notes on what was happening to me and to the squad. Bob figured that once I snapped out of it, I would want to know.

According to Bob's notes, the time of the mortar attack was about 7:00 P.M. It was also mentioned that after I was dragged to the gun, I couldn't help with anything. Travis was dropping rounds down the tube, while I lay in the corner, not even covering my ears. When the fire mission was finally over, I had to be helped to my bunker. I wouldn't lie down, instead I crawled to a corner and started talking more and more deliriously. I was sick to my stomach, and the corpsman wasn't able to see me until morning.

When the corpsman found me, I was walking around the area where Bruce was killed, still partly in shock from his death. The squad was worried about me and so was the corpsman. They thought I would have to be sent back to the rear to get more help. The corpsman was treating my left eye for a bad infection. Bob was told that something must have bit me, and the infection affected my eye. I was also being treated for sores on my face, the start of jungle rot. Jungle rot makes sores on the body that, if infected, could leave scars. Also, it can spread to any part of your body.

It was now July 28, and Bob went with me to the battalion aid station. I was starting to come out of it, but my eye was still giving me trouble. I had to wear a patch over it for days.

Bob also had been saving my mail for me, and he thought that today would be a good time for me to read some letters from home. I had a hard time because I was still wearing the patch. Bob then gave me the notes he was keeping, but told me not to read them unless I was ready to join the squad and start carrying my load again. He also said that we all need each other's help, and the only way we might get to go home is if we keep pushing on, fighting this nightmare all the way. I knew Bob didn't want to sound so hard, but he wanted me to realize that unless I got completely over the shock of Largo, it would be only a matter of time before I ended up the same way.

It was now August 1, and I was back doing something useful again. The squad, along with Bob, had done wonders for me. I was now getting in more practice as a gunner, because I was next in line.

It was also getting close to my birthday, and I was receiving packages and birthday cards. One of the packages contained a cake from my sister Carol. Soon I would be twenty years old, yet I felt and looked as if I was thirty.

On the morning of my birthday, we were awakened by incoming rounds. They just lasted long enough to harass us and keep us uptight the rest of the day. We stayed in our bunkers and holes a lot, so the one thing we could do was write letters. It helped keep our minds off this place. When we did go out of our bunkers, we hung around the mortar, cleaning it up and making sure we had plenty of ammo for fire missions.

Most of the time we lived like rats, buried in the corner of our bunkers, hugging the ground, and wishing we could go deeper. We'd been getting hit steadily for the last five days, sometimes early in the morning, and sometimes as soon as it got dark. Usually an attack lasts about three hours. One night the Vietcong would hit us with rockets, and another night with mortars and artillery. It's a shame, because we have our jets constantly flying over, but they can't seem to spot a damn thing. Most of our fire missions last all day and sometimes through the night. The grunts report that they find some dead Vietcong outside of our perimeter.

What good are a few dead Vietcong, compared to the good marines we've lost? During the day the grunts go on sweeps near the DMZ, and never see the Vietcong. They blow up cave after cave, while we mortarmen hammer away at a mountainside, with hundreds and hundreds of rounds. Usually, we don't find a damn thing.

Con Thien is one of the places known as "Leatherneck Square." The other places that make up the square are Camp Carroll, Gio Lihn, and Dong Ha. If the Vietcong could get the marines out of these places, they would have their paradise back.

It was now the tenth of August, and church services were being held. Marines from different religious backgrounds gathered under one tent and prayed to God. We all knew that He was the only one that could get us out of this mess and back home. When I got back to the area, I was told that in the morning I would be going to Dong Ha. Every once in a while, one man from each squad gets to go back to the rear area to pick up the personal needs of the squad, such as writing material, shaving cream, blades, soap, and so on. It also gives a marine a chance to get some cold beer, take in a movie, and get a couple of nights of good sleep before returning to the field.

In the morning, I waited for the convoy. When I got to Dong Ha, it was still early, so I picked up the things the squad needed and took them back to the place I would be staying at for a few days. I spent the rest of the evening at the club.

The next day I had one more important thing to do: I turned in my rifle and drew a pistol with a holster and a K-bar. Gunners and A-gunners did not carry rifles, just .45 caliber pistols. When I finished with that, I bought some mirrors and candles from the Vietnamese area. At night, I went back to the club and then took in a movie, an outdoor-type movie.

It was early when I caught the convoy back to Con Thien. When the trucks got near we started getting incoming rounds from mortars. Since the trucks made easy targets, the drivers waited with the supplies while the rest of the marines and I made it back to our sections. After a few fire missions the incoming stopped, and our supplies were brought in. The important thing was that there was enough beer for everyone.

In the morning I helped the squad build some racks in the old ammo bunker. We only had one fire mission. Since the day was pretty quiet, I dug out my camera and started taking some pictures of Con Thien. The lieutenant came around and told us that the guys that were wounded on the night Bruce was killed would not be coming back to Vietnam. He said they would be staying in Okinawa until they get their orders to go back to the States.

I started thinking of the original section I was in when I first got to this country. There are only seven guys left from the first section, since February. The rest are all new replacements. After taking a few more pictures, I went back to the bunker and wrote home.

Today is Saturday, August 26. It's been raining hard off and on for the past week. I guess the monsoon season is starting early; what a miserable six months this is going to be. The marines hate this weather, but it seems the

Vietcong love it. It's their paradise, not ours! This country has some rain forests, but most of the area has been turned into rice paddies, which are flooded throughout the northeast. The rice fields are normally made up into a number of square paddies, and from the air they look like a checkerboard. These paddies are constructed with dirt dikes separating them so that they can be kept flooded. The rice paddies will usually have mud and water one to two feet deep, making it very difficult for us to cross. Every time we cross these fields, we pray the operation will not be a critical one. Even the dirt roads are water holes, and as soon as we set up our gun pits, they, too, become waterholes.

The sugarcane fields are also in the Vietcong's favor. When the cane is fully grown it offers excellent concealment, of which the Vietcong take advantage. Once inside the cane field, the Vietcong can see real well into the outside without being seen themselves. This is perfect for their snipers and very dangerous for us.

Another important thing about this mess is that the trees are close together, overgrown with vines and dense brush. The Vietcong are quite small and know this paradise well, therefore, they can move through these areas without being noticed. The chances of them being ambushed are quite low.

Everything gets tied up in the monsoon season. Our helicopters bring in our water and food every chance they get, but when it rains hard, they just can't fly in. Oh God! What a place!

Sometime ago I wrote a letter home asking for socks. One of the things a marine needs over here in the monsoon season is plenty of socks. The package hasn't arrived yet, but I'm hoping it will any day now. Meanwhile, the letter went something like this:

Dear Ma and Dad,

There is something I must ask for. I need socks! I don't care what color they are, and you don't have to buy any. Just send me my old ones, because I can't get any socks over here. I'd even wear my sister Joyce's socks, and if they were nylons, I'd wear two pair.

Right now I have two pairs of socks left. One pair is outside hanging on the barbed wire, but they are wet and muddy. They will not dry because the sun hasn't been out in eight days now. My other pair is on my feet. They are also wet and muddy, but I've only had them on for six days. The socks are what I need in a hurry, and I would appreciate them very much. Thanks!

Your loving, miserable son,
Mike

The twenty-eighth of August was another day to spend in our bunkers. We took over 170 rounds of incoming for the whole day.

The Vietcong were hitting us with artillery that had delayed fuses, which is some bad stuff. It seemed like every time we had our B-52s bomb the hell out of an area in North Vietnam, the Vietcong would throw everything they had back at us. What a feeling it is to sit in your bunker like a sitting duck and hope the bunker doesn't take a direct hit.

We needed another bunker in the compound, so we started building, and every night the Vietcong hit us with incoming rounds. Friday marked our fiftieth day at Con Thien. The boys at Dong Ha took a chance and flew us in hot chow. Some of the fellows celebrated by playing a game of Monopoly, but before anybody could buy Boardwalk or Park Place, the game was interrupted by a fire mission. The fire mission only lasted a little while, but it was long enough so that nobody wanted to finish Monopoly.

As the marines climbed into the racks that night, I'm sure a lot of them felt the way I did. I was glad and thankful to still be alive.

It was now Saturday, September 2, and it was time for the marines to head back to Dong Ha. There they would wait for their flight out of this country. Everybody looked forward to that day. While Bill and I were at the landing zone, the Vietcong mortared the hell out of Con Thien. All the helicopters took off except for one, because that chopper pilot got the word that a badly wounded marine was being brought to the landing zone. Bill and I ran to help carry the stretcher. It was Sal Salone. He was in the same section as Bill and was a good friend of both of us. Sal was hit by a mortar, and his stomach was half gone. Bill and I carried him into the chopper and then got the hell back to our sections.

The last thing Bill and I heard about Sal was that he made it. Sal was being held together with tubing on a hospital ship. What an awful price to pay!

The Vietcong still kept hitting us throughout the day, everyday. Bill was slightly wounded the day after Sal got his. The rounds have been hitting all around us, and we've been losing a lot of marines. Our buddies are dropping all over, and it's a wonder we don't have more marines losing their cool.

Nobody knows where that first round is going to hit, and it only takes one.

The word finally came down that our battalion is moving out of this hellhole. It's Saturday, September 9 and we've been here a total of fifty-nine days. This is the longest time any battalion has stayed at Con Thien. When we did move out we humped about 2,000 meters, and then caught trucks to a place called Cam Lo Hill.

There was hot chow waiting for us, and this gave us the feeling we wouldn't be here long.

It was just about time to get some sleep when I realized that today was also my anniversary. I've been in for one year today, and I have sure grown up some.

It was morning before we knew it and time to move out again. This time we humped to Cam Lo bridge and when we got there, the CBS cameramen were waiting to take pictures. The word we got from them was that they wanted to see the battalion that spent so many days on Con Thien. This is the same place I was assigned to when I joined the first section way back in February.

We were told to start building our hootches and then fill sandbags for the ammo bunker and gunpit. I also became the acting squad leader.

On Wednesday I brought my laundry down to where the villagers washed their clothes. I gave the big bag to some pretty little girls, and it only cost a dollar for the whole bag.

It's been raining for over a week now, only stopping for short intervals. None of us seem to mind the rain, because now we can at least breath a little easier. It also gives us a chance to catch up on our letter writing.

There hasn't been much Vietcong activity, now that the monsoon season is in full swing. Everything is slowing down. When we're not writing letters, we're cleaning our weapons. We also clean the mortar and wipe it dry every chance we get, so the baby doesn't rust out.

It's now Sunday, September 17, and no mail came in again. It's been raining like hell and the river has risen higher than it's ever been before.

Jerry and I stayed in the hootch most of the day and talked about being home. When it got dark I kicked off my boots and lay back on my rubber mattress. Then I waited for another night to pass in Vietnam.

It was two in the morning when I rolled over and couldn't believe my eyes. My boots were bobbing up and down in water. I shook Jerry and when he woke up, I told him that we were afloat. It wasn't a lie, either. The river had risen up over the land, and we were now in two feet of water. We pulled our boots on and when I went to the FDC bunker, Jerry awakened the rest of the guys.

Corporal Croto was on duty but was not aware of the flooding. The water had not reached the huge chair he was sitting on nor the cots that the sergeant and the other corporals were sleeping on. I shook the sergeant, since he was top dog right then, and he took one look and got on the radio. It was never admitted by Corporal Croto that he might have fallen asleep, but I'm sure winks were in order for him, to not notice the water rising. The lieutenant was at the other end of the radio giving us orders to pack up and make our way to the hill. He would be sending a squad of grunts to meet us.

All we were able to take with us were our weapons and the mortar. I was the gunner so I was elected to carry the bipods. By this time the water reached up to our waist. The thirteen of us headed toward what looked like the gates of the compound. Our strict orders were to hold onto each other's flak jacket and not to let go for any reason. When we came to places where the land dipped, the water was chest high—my chest, not the fellows that were 6'1" or 6'2", but mine. This was one time where being tall was beautiful.

The water had been rushing over the land with a current as strong as I have ever witnessed before. I was the second one from the end, holding on for my life. We were about halfway to the hill, praying for an incline in the land, when we heard a marine yelling for his life. It was one of the grunts from Lima Company. He was in deep water, hung up on barbed wire. The wire kept pulling him down. The lieutenant from Lima Company told us to stay put and not break the human chain. The marine was too far from us; we needed some rope. Time was running out, and there wasn't rope or anything to help the poor soul, so the lieutenant broke away and went after him. He was like a feather in the current, tumbling through the water right past the drowning marine. It was the last effort, because the screaming stopped. His nightmares of this war would be no more. Thirteen of us, plus some of the grunts 100 yards away, watched him go under, and now that too is part of our bad dreams. As for the lieutenant, none of us knew that night if he made it to safety.

In all this confusion and yelling, there wasn't a Vietcong to be seen. They were busy looking for high ground themselves.

At this time of the night, we were hooked up with the grunts and started our uphill walk.

Nobody knew the exact time, but it wasn't light out yet. The illumination rounds were still going off, lighting up the whole area.

One of the rounds landed in the open cab of a crane some distance away. It was like a bolt of lightening coming from the crane, and flames were shooting out. We didn't know any more about that until we got to the top of the hill. The word passed around that an engineer was electrocuted in the crane. Now I'm sure that fellow had good reason for being in that spot at that time, but what a horrible way to die.

We couldn't get dried out, but some of the fellows managed to get dry cigarettes off the villagers. The ones that didn't smoke, like myself, fed our faces.

Our weapons and the mortar needed a good drying

out, and also a good cleaning, but the rain kept on coming.

It was another whole day before we found out how many casualties there had been. Including the engineer, the grunt from Lima Company, and the lieutenant (whom they found a day and half later, his body swollen like a balloon), there were six other marines that died that night. Not one damn shot was fired.

It was a couple of days more before any of us could go back to the bridge and salvage our gear. It was a total of ten days before we actually went back to guard the bridge. One of the buildings where we had good observation was a three story cement slab. This was also the only building that saved the lives of three grunts during the flood. They had gone on the roof and waited for choppers, and the water didn't get any further than the second level. By this time the Vietcong had dried out also and started throwing their mortars at us again. It was like clockwork; every night as soon as it got dark, we would get incoming rounds.

Every time I dove for my hole or ran into a bunker, I carried the thought of Bruce with me. Sure, I made it through the flood and lived through several more mortar attacks, but how much more of this could I take?

Is it just a matter of time, and is this the way Bruce felt before he got it? I was coming apart inside again, but I was hoping it didn't show. Oh, how I'm fighting this! I felt that with Bruce gone, there was nobody over here to look out for me anymore. I never had to live with this kind of fear before, and now in one more week I'll be a squad leader, responsible for six other marines. I have to get my head together, so I can set them a good image of a leader.

Most importantly, God, I don't want to get these men killed. Please help me get through another night.

Chapter IX

Friday, October 6: Today seven happy marines leave for Dong Ha. Soon they will be on their way home. Every time I see the fellows leaving, I can't help wishing it was me that's going home. I guess the system is fair by having every marine spend thirteen months over here before going back to the States. Yes, it's fair all right, as long as you're able to go home in one piece. I'd hate to tell the parents or the wife of a dead marine that this system, or any part of this war, is fair.

The convoy that was taking these fellows to Dong Ha was also bringing in our mail. Benson had been on the convoy also. He was a new marine in the mortar platoon but had been given a chance to pick up some personal needs for the platoon. One of the things he brought back for himself was a portable tape player.

He loved to listen to soul music. A couple of the other new marines enjoyed playing cards, so there were a few occasions where I joined in on a good card game. It does take your mind off things, especially when you win.

One morning while we were building some wash racks for our clothes, we put together a nice looking card table out of ammo boxes.

One of the routine tasks we do every morning, or the first chance we're able to get to it, is clean the mortar. We also put oil on it to keep it from rusting. Then we made sure we had plenty of ammo in the bunker. The rest of the day is sometimes planned by Charlie. There were a couple of times when I started to write a letter to Bruce's parents, but ended up throwing the letter away. It just seemed that the words didn't want to come out right. It's been over a month now since the tragic night, and I knew that a letter had to be written by me. I wanted to tell them how I felt about Bruce and that I also knew what a remarkable son he was. The letter didn't get written that day, but I knew it had to be done soon.

A few days passed, and when mail came in I received a large envelope with the pictures of Okinawa in it. They were the ones taken of the ceremony for the VIPs. Bruce was in a few of them, and he looked real good. I was certain now that I would be able to get that letter off to his parents, and enclose one of these pictures of their son. Before I sealed the envelope, I asked almost every marine in the section who knew Bruce if he would like to say something and sign his name. They really came through for me, because before they were finished, the envelope I had for the letter was no good anymore. The letter was done, all fifteen pages of it.

It was now Sunday, October 15, and a few of us fellows went for a water run. It doesn't involve much, but it has to get done. We loaded the empty cans on back of the flat bed, put our flak jackets on, and hopped in the back. We didn't have very far to go, but there was sniper fire from time to time.

I was squad leader now, but I didn't feel any kind of difference at this time. Bob Saufo and I were pretty close now, but he was our wireman, and he kept pretty busy. He would also be leaving for the rear area soon, and that meant a lot of the fellows that were in the platoon back in Okinawa would be gone then.

On Friday, October 20, four more marines left for Dong Ha. It was also the forty-second day that we had been in the Cam Lo area. During the early hours of morning on the twenty-first, the squad fired mortar rounds for harassment and illumination. These rounds are called H and I's.

We got the word that there was some kind of Vietcong election going on, and it might be pretty quiet until it's all over.

One of the good things about this area was that we were able to sleep on cots in tents, instead of on racks built inside of bunkers. The holes and trenches were nearby and were used quite a lot, but we didn't have to eat, sleep, and live in them for twenty-four hours a day. In this particular area, everything but the showers and shitters were under a tent. The aid station, the worship services, and the mess hall were under a tent. Sandbags had been built up on all four sides.

One morning while our cooks were preparing breakfast, a stove fell over, shooting flames up in the tent, which caught fire. The platoon was called to put it out. We didn't want to waste much of our water, so we threw sand on it. The tent was damaged, but not so badly that it couldn't be used for anything. The main thing is that not one man got burned.

Another day when we were not putting out fires, we got together a game of tackle football, in the mud, of course. It was something else to keep our minds off this war.

We also had police calls, which means cleaning up the area. It involved all of the 81 mortar platoon, and it covered the entire perimeter.

There were times when we didn't feel like doing anything, not playing cards or football. It seemed that on these days, we ended up unloading trucks full of ammo, and it usually rained while we were doing it.

On Wednesday, October 25, two of our mortar sections switched places. We stayed put, because I guess it wasn't our turn to change the scenery. This same day I went down to the village to pick up my laundry. I wasn't supposed to go alone, but I knew there were some marines already down there. It was a friendly village, but you had to be careful just the same. Nobody could be sure about Papa San. The fact was that he might stick a knife in your back for looking at his nine-year-old daughter. Another important fact was that if you ate anything they sold, you were a fool.

Some of them felt that if they poisoned you, it would be like saying, "Thank you for screwing up our homeland." Fifteen minutes was really all the time a marine needed down at the village. This gave other marines time to look around for whatever junk they might want to buy.

The next morning the section leader passed the word to the squad leaders that he wanted our 782 gear cleaned up. He was coming around to inspect it. It was the first inspection of this kind since I entered Vietnam. I think mainly it was to see how raggedy our gear was and to get it replaced if need be. Our weapons were checked weekly, and the mortar was checked every day.

I was hoping I would be able to keep my helmet liner, because I had been keeping a calendar of months on it. I was marking the time I had to stay in Vietnam with a black felt-tip marker. It was the helmet I had from the beginning, and I sort of got attached to it. The section leader walked through with the lieutenant, and the inspection was over in a matter of minutes.

Friday came, and it was time to police the whole area again. More new replacements arrived and, to them, cleaning up the area seemed very petty stuff to be doing in Vietnam. Once they're here a while in Charlie's paradise, they will have a better picture of why we do the things we do.

The next morning marked our fiftieth day in the Cam

Lo area. I was sitting in the tent cleaning my .45 caliber when the word came down that the lieutenant wanted to see me. I figured it had to be important, so I wasted no time. Out of the tent I went, across the muddy road and up some stairs made out of wooden ammo boxes. When I got there he told me that I had the chance to go to Hawaii for my R&R, which means rest and relaxation. He had to have my answer right away.

I was respectful to him when I told him no thanks, but then thanked him for keeping me in mind. The lieutenant looked surprised but nevertheless got back on the radio and passed the message along. The lieutenant noticed that I had put in for the R&R at Sydney, Australia, but he said that there is no guarantee I would get that spot. I said I realized this, but was eligible for R&R after six months in this country, and I'm pushing almost ten months now. I guess I could wait a little longer to see what else comes along. I don't think the lieutenant understood why I felt this way or why I turned down Hawaii, but he said he would do what he could and get back to me. I left his headquarters, without showing him anymore of my feelings.

Now God knew that I needed R&R, and I knew that I was overdue in this damn war. I felt like a lot of other marines in some ways. We're over here fighting a war in a country where we don't even feel wanted by the people we're helping. We go along with the system day in and day out, and sometimes we want a little bit more than what the system is willing to give. Sometimes it's difficult to settle for less. We want what we want!

It was only a short time later when I was really thrown into a bad mood. I found out from Bob, who just happened to have a very good friend in Communications, that one spot did come down for Australia, but it had been taken by another lieutenant attached to the grunt companies. The real pisser was that he had been in Vietnam four months less than I.

By this time I had to find a place to cool off. Bob and I went down to the stream; I took off my boots, socks, and belt and went for a swim. Bob stood nearby with our weapons. The big letdown would soon pass.

On Sunday, the morning started off with us filling sandbags. When the break in the routine came, I gathered my laundry up and brought it to one of the Vietnamese children. Then I walked over to say good-bye to some of the other lucky marines. Their orders read that they were going home. When I got back to my squad's tent the lieutenant was there looking for me. He said, "Son, how does Tokyo, Japan sound to you?" I said, "Not bad, Sir. When would I leave?" He went on to say that I could leave on the very next convoy to Dong Ha. Those were the magic words I wanted to hear, especially when I was still thinking about the other fellows leaving. It wasn't homeward-bound for me, but it was out of this country and for the same length of time as Australia would have been. One of the big reasons I wanted Australia was that I wanted to see girls with round eyes. All in all, it's been almost a year now since I saw some. Oh, well!

Tokyo Rose, here I come.

Chapter X

Have you ever tried to pack your suitcase in a hurry and borrow money from somebody at the same time? That was my first time. There I was, throwing stuff in my seabag and asking everybody in the tent for money. I had some saved but I knew I needed more. It was as if I expected them to come running over and empty their pockets in the bag. I really didn't want it that way, but I guess that's the way it looked to them. As it was, the fellows came through, like they always came through. They knew, and so did I, that I would pay back every dollar if I was able to. I didn't dwell on that thought too long.

After spending a quiet night in Dong Ha, I was flown to Danang. I checked my orders in and then looked around in the PX.

I met a grunt whose name was Al, and even when we got drunk that night, it was an easy name to remember. I met up with another marine whose name was Ray. He was the same fellow that Bruce tangled with back in January or February. Ray didn't turn out to be that bad of a marine; he was just one that I couldn't find myself getting close to. Even that night at the club would have been something more than peaceful if it wasn't for Al.

The next day we were hung over. It was the first time since Okinawa that I had gotten drunk.

The flight to Tokyo was an afternoon flight, and it took about five and a half hours.

From the airport, we were taken by way of bus to Camp Sama, the R&R center.

If a guy wanted to save all the money he came with, this place was great. Free room and board, plenty of food, and a lot of the same stuff you would find at any military base.

Al and I felt the same way; we had to get out of here really early in the morning.

Before we left, a third marine joined us. His name was John. The three of us found the bus station and headed out for Yokahama.

It was 8:00 A.M. when we dropped our duffle bags off at a place called the Central Hotel. I had just under three hundred dollars left. I hoped that it would last six more days. It wasn't very long at all until the three of us were arm in arm with three geisha girls. They were all friends. Two of them lived close; the one I picked didn't.

Their names were Mari, Paunki, and Cozaco. Since everybody had different plans at this particular time, we split up. It wasn't really the smartest thing to do, because now we had to be very careful. The three of us marines were alone in a big place with no one that could speak English.

Mari and I took a cab, and she showed me her place. That night we had dinner at a fancy restaurant.

In the morning I noticed that Mari's place was near the Navy exchange. I needed a few things, so we walked over and looked around.

At night we went shopping and her eyes landed on a pair of go-go boots. At that time I felt that to buy her the boots was the least thing I could do. I bought the boots and then we hit a few bars. We went from the bars to the stores and her eyes were getting bigger all the time, while mine were getting more bloodshot. The few things she was able to say perfectly were "Buy me that, give me this," or "Give me that, buy me this." I was sure she had me confused with a sailor who had just gotten off the boat. I was feeling drunk, but not so bad that I didn't know how to spend money. I couldn't help wondering if John and Al were going through this same shit.

I finally got across to her that we should go see my friends John and Al. Tomorrow, very early, would do. I think she also knew that I was tired of this adventure.

The next day, just like clockwork, a cab picked us up in front of Mari's house and stopped in front of Paunki's place. I got out and motioned to Mari to come with me. The cab driver wouldn't take my money and Mari wouldn't get out. She pointed to the house and the cab drove off with her still in it.

That was real great. Now I felt like the odd-man-out. After telling John the facts, the five of us went into Tokyo.

We put together a wild party at night and took stupid pictures, while getting stoned on saki.

The next day I didn't know where I was until somebody gave me a clue. Later John, Paunki, and myself went back to Mari's place to pick up my bag. I went in alone and she was getting ready to go out. Once I had the bag in my hand she understood the rest. She stopped me at the door, opened a dresser drawer, and handed me a swinger camera. I put the camera down, but she insisted I keep it. She had tears in her eyes when she handed the camera to me again. I didn't fully understand any of this, the camera, or the tears. My mind was a blur, like so many other times. I kissed her once, walked away, and never looked back. Many times though, I wondered about what else I could have done.

I played the solo routine for the rest of the day, but at night John and Al wanted to go to Club Zebra. It was a great-looking club, but it was for couples only, which meant I needed an escort fast. There were plenty of

Japanese girls out in front, but Paunki wanted to surprise me by taking me to another club where another one of her friends worked. When we got to the front door, Paunki told us that it would be better to wait outside. She came back out with her friend Midore, to see if I was still anxious about this whole deal. I certainly was, but I never knew how Paunki was able to talk the owner of the bar into letting Midore off the rest of the night.

After a fun night at Club Zebra, the six of us found ourselves splitting up again. It was to be the last night in Tokyo. The next morning after breakfast, Midore and I met with John and Paunki.

We took some pictures and then said our good-byes. Al and Cozaco were not home when John went by earlier, so we figured Al would show up sooner or later at Camp Sama. It was tough leaving, as it always is, but John and I had plans of calling home from Camp Sama, and tonight would be the only chance. We knew it would be some kind of surprise to our folks.

Seven days had not nearly been long enough and soon we would be back in the war, trying to stay alive.

On November 9, we landed back in Da Nang from Tokyo. The first thing we had to do was to get out of our civilian clothes and back into our utilities. Later on, I stopped at the PX and then took in a movie. The movie was called *Texas Across the River*, starring Dean Martin.

The next day was spent in the Seabee's area. It was the Marine Corps' birthday, but it still felt like any other day.

When we landed in Dong Ha, John and Al went back to the grunt companies. I picked up my .45 caliber and then went to find out where I would be sleeping tonight.

The section that I was in was still at Cam Lo hill. I'll be leaving on the next convoy. It wasn't great to get back, but it was great to see my buddies. My mail had been coming in all along, and it was being held at headquarters. The sergeant told me to go along with another marine to pick up the squad's mail. He said, "Half the mail is probably yours anyway."

The sergeant wasn't far off; when we got back to the squad tent and all the mail was sorted, I had a total of fifty-six letters and four packages. What a welcome back that was.

I tore open the packages first and passed the goodies around. Talk about having friends.

It took me two days to finally read the letters, because of all the normal duties and working parties that had to get done. I don't recall how long it took me to answer all those letters, but I did get it accomplished.

It was Tuesday now, and boy, was I tired from the night before. I was firing illumination rounds every ten minutes for four hours. When I had some free time I was either writing letters or catching up on my sleep. The next day the supply truck came, and we bought only the things we really needed, because the word came around again that we pack up tonight and move out of this place in the morning.

That always made us worry more, not knowing where we're heading or what the hell we might run into. Morning came fast as it always does, and just as we were about to move out, a chopper brought us our mail and more C-rations. They were passed out, and we were told not to read our mail until we got where we were going. I don't know what the other fellows thought at that instant but the idea of me getting wounded or killed before I read my mail made me quiver. We were now on our way to a place they call Checkpoint Two.

It wasn't very far, and when we got there, we broke

open the C-rations and started chowing down. Some were eating, others were reading their mail, and I was doing a little of both.

As soon as it got dark, some Vietcong activity must have been spotted, because the forward observer called for a fire mission. Every mortar gun responded, and each gun dropped ten rounds before the command came over loud and clear to cease fire.

We knew the rounds were hitting close by, but that's what was called for. The word finally came back to us that the rounds landed on one of our grunt companies that was dug in. It was obvious that it was a blown fire mission, and we prayed that we didn't waste the lives of our own men. I'm sure somebody may have known the outcome of that night, but as for myself and the fellows in the mortar section, we were kept in the dark. I didn't hear of any marines being wounded or any fatalities.

Friday, November 17, the mortars and the bunkers needed some work done on them. The baseplates on all the guns were sunk deep in the ground from the night before. We dug them up, and then seated them again properly. We cleaned the rest of the area, and then started filling some sand bags. The night was quiet.

The next day our planes were flying low over the whole area. We found out that they were dropping gas on the Vietcong, which seemed to be a great idea at the time. However, some of the gas was dropped a little too close for comfort, and the wind carried it to our perimeter. It caught us off guard, and had the whole platoon scrambling for gas masks. It did pass over, but for a while it really shook our shit, because we did catch a good part of the gas. Nobody was injured, but our insides and nostrils were fairly cleaned out now.

It seemed to us by this time that we didn't need the

Vietcong to give us any trouble; we were doing a good job of that ourselves. All in all, what's happened is still only one aspect of war.

Six days have passed since our arrival here. We kept busy in the day building the bunkers better while the grunts were sent out on patrols with little contact from Charlie. Just after dark they would let loose with the mortars and rockets. Then we would send back our mortars, both sides hoping to harass or cause as much damage as possible. This stuff went on for days. In the meantime more and more of my buddies were heading home. Their time was up. New replacements had been coming in all along, which meant now I had only one other man in my squad that had been in Vietnam over six months. Also, with the replacements came three brand new mortar guns for the platoon.

Thanksgiving Day came and went, and it was a far cry from how I spent my last one. On one of the rainy days we had, the gunnery sergeant called a meeting of squad leaders. He passed out some squad record books and told us to use them for something besides writing gear. He also discussed that as soon as the rain lets up, we would be prep firing the mortars for one of our grunt companies. Charlie was certainly nearby, but they wanted us to come to them.

I noticed that some of the new guys were feeling kind of down. I knew it was because they weren't receiving their mail. Some of them would have given up their food or a night's sleep to read a letter from their wife or girl.

It's just a fact; when it rains a lot, everything gets backed up.

I managed to finally write Kincannon a letter, even though the letter wouldn't get out for a few days. Kincannon was home now and out of the marines. I was hoping things back home would settle him down. Kincannon went through some kind of hell the night Bruce got it.

It was December 8, when a new lieutenant joined our platoon. Bob and I were down by the ammo bunker getting ready to fire illumination rounds. The convoy from Dong Ha came up just before it was getting dark, and the lieutenant had been on one of the trucks. After he met the gunnery sergeant and some of the other marines, he came down by the mortar, introduced himself, and started asking Bob and me some questions about the mortar. I passed his little quiz. After four questions, Bob, with an impatient look, said, "Sir, I'm the platoon wireman and not a mortarman." Bob never did hit it off with the lieutenant after that. I guess it was my turn again, because before he left us, he reminded me that I should use the word Sir when talking to a lieutenant in the United States Marine Corps.

I told him that I was sure I could get better at it, it's just that I was out of practice since being over here. One final wish was said, and that was that he expected his men in his platoon to render a salute to him, upon seeing him for the first time each day. This lieutenant wasn't kidding either; he had to be only twenty-one years old, and I felt as if I was over the hill already. With a little over three months to go, I wasn't looking forward to this sudden adjustment.

One of the early projects that had to be done was building a new command post bunker. This would have to be made big enough for four people—the lieutenant, the gunnery sergeant, the platoon sergeant, and the ammo corporal. Another project was a walkway made from ammo boxes.

It was now Sunday, December 10 and time for another malaria pill. You can always tell it's Sunday, because the corporal comes around with this pink pill made for a horse. This date also marked the twenty-fifth day at Checkpoint Two.

The next morning, the fourth section was picked to be on standby for the Second Battalion Fourth Marines. The operation was near Dong Ha, so the trucks came and picked up the fourth section.

The operation only lasted three days. Shortly after the convoy brought the fourth section back, a chopper landed and a chaplain got out. I guess the VIPs wanted the men to hear a church service. The rumor was that we were supposed to hear one once a week, but we were lucky if we heard one once a month.

The chaplain had some time before the chopper came to pick him up, so he made some of us fellows feel good by just talking with us. He told us that before he left Dong Ha the weather was fifty-six degrees. This was at one in the afternoon, so you can imagine how cold it gets at night and in the early morning.

It's now Friday, December 15, and today makes my tenth month in Charlie's paradise.

Vietcong activity had been slight in this area, which gave us a much-needed rest and a string of days where we could take showers with hot water. The lieutenant wanted the squads to run gun drill, so we could stay sharp. On one of the days we were running a gun drill, three choppers came in, and a very important figure stepped out. It was General Westmoreland.

Up to this point, I had only heard about him, but today I saw him up close. The choppers stood waiting, because it was to be a very short visit. The general walked around and looked in a few of the bunkers and asked some of the marines how they were getting along. He also asked if they were getting enough food and supplies. You can be sure those marines thought about the questions before they answered. It lasted only about ten minutes, and the general was gone.

A couple of more days passed, and the new lieutenant sent word that he wanted to see me.

When I got to his bunker, the gunnery sergeant told me to sit down, but he had a smile on his face when he said this. The lieutenant then came over and told me that I was picked for an in-country R&R. It was hard for me to believe what I was hearing. He went on to say, "One spot came through, and from what the gunnery tells me, along with the other sergeants and corporals, you warrant the right to go."

He told me things I already knew, such as the fact that I've been over here ten months and haven't missed any operations, and I have somebody capable of running my squad while I am gone. It was great to hear this coming from the lieutenant. I was honored and very thankful. God had to be looking out for me. The lieutenant said that I would be leaving in the morning for Dong Ha and arrive back here on the fourth day.

He was pretty sure the platoon would not go anywhere until after Christmas. I thanked him and the gunnery sergeant again and went back to my bunker.

I still couldn't help thinking about how lucky a marine I was. I had only been back in the field a little over a month and already was given another chance away from the war.

Da Nang is where the marines in this area go for an in-country R&R. It's one of our larger bases in Vietnam. It's well protected, which means a good place to lay your head down. The base could get hit with incoming rounds, and if you were in another part of the base, you wouldn't be in too much danger. Time just zipped by, but I made the best of every hour. Once in Da Nang, I took a bus to

China Beach. At least the Vietnamese are proud to call it a bus. This place had quite a lot: movies, live entertainment, cold beer, booze, and girls. Again, not necessarily in that order.

When I checked in, I was given one sheet, one blanket, and a pillowcase. I went over to the hut, threw what little stuff I had on a bunk and went right to the club. Later that night, I took in a live show.

The next day my luck was still holding; Bob Hope and Raquel Welsh were over here with the USO show. I was standing quite a ways back, but the show was great. I saw a couple of shows more, and two movies, *One Spy Too Many* and *Rough Night in Jericho*.

I was exhausted when I got back to the hut that night. About 12:30 A.M. the Da Nang airstrip was hit with some rockets. Nobody was hurt.

Before I checked out of China Beach, I stopped at the PX store. I picked up as much stuff as I thought would last the rest of my time in Vietnam, writing gear, soap, toothpaste, et cetera. I caught the plane to Dong Ha and then went over to check on the platoon's mail. I'll be bringing the mail back with me on the next convoy.

The R&R had been good, very good, but I was glad I was back in time for Christmas. If I couldn't be with my family, the next best thing was being among my buddies.

Everything was the same when I got back.

It was Christmas Eve, and the squad was up early to get ready for a lot of fire missions. The cease-fire agreement was set to go at 1800. That's 6:00 P.M. civilian time.

It will be in effect until 6:00 P.M. Christmas day. We fired the mortars continually, and when that hour came, our gun alone fired seventy-eight rounds.

Most of the men in the platoon turned in for the night early and took advantage of the quiet hours.

Christmas in Vietnam was like everybody expected, just another lousy day. It was also our fortieth day at this place. Our minds are on the operation tomorrow. All we know about this one so far is that choppers will be here for us in the morning.

When the new day came, I quickly found out that our destination was Dong Ha. From there we pull the operation. The only thing I could find out from the gunny was that we were supposed to land in an unmarked area and then finish the operation on foot. The reason we went to Dong Ha first is because somebody felt we needed some special choppers alongside us. These choppers were known as gun ships.

The gunny said, "They certainly help when you come across some shit." I told him that if I had a choice in the matter, I'd rather walk into shit than land in it. I don't know if he agreed, but I got a laugh out of him.

Chapter XI

This operation was no different than the rest. I was always uneasy during operations. While I was sitting in the chopper, headed for this unmarked area, I was watching the faces of some of the new replacements. I was trying to read their minds. I was wondering if their thoughts were on their loved ones or on what they were going to do when Charlie starts shooting at us. One of the things I learned quickly over here was that when you get this close to action, your mind has to be right there on what you're doing, or you could end up going home in a plastic bag.

We were just minutes away now, and my stomach was tight as knots. I wanted to shake the bad thoughts, but I couldn't. I asked myself *who's coming back from this operation, or the next one we pull, or the one after that?* The chopper touched down, the back opened, and the gunny yelled "Move, move, move." My very next thought was *Oh shit!* I was the third one out, and led my squad away from the choppers and to what little cover there was. We lay there waiting for the order to move, while the choppers took off.

It was quiet now, so damn quiet. Charlie knew we were here all right, but the Vietcong wanted it their way. Their best game was hit and run.

We walked to the area where we were to get our first night's rest, and the first thing we did was to get the mortars set up. Our water supply was good, but just in case we needed some, a river was only seventy-five feet away.

Each squad dug their gun pits before their own fox holes or trenches. Before the holes were the way we wanted them or as deep as we would have liked them, Charlie let loose with some sixty-milimeter mortar rounds. It wasn't enough to give away their position, just enough rounds to let us know they were definitely out there.

The next day it rained, and since there was nothing special going on, we stayed under our hootches to keep dry as possible. The hootches were made from our shelter halves and ponchos.

The one time the rain let up, we were cleaning up the area, and we took some sniper rounds. Nobody was hit, but it made us want to go after the Vietcong that much faster.

The next day we cleaned our rifles, and then I took my squad down to the water point. One squad at a time went. Everybody took their turns standing guard, while the others washed up and shaved. It was New Year's Eve, and another cease-fire was set to go, again at 1800.

Before we knew it, a new year was here. January 1, 1968.

We moved on to another location and started building our gun pits all over again. We had hot chow flown in to us, and I also received a check for $151. They usually try to pay us at the beginning of each month. Most of the fellows, including myself, send their money home, unless they have an R&R coming up soon.

The next morning was our eighth day in the bush, and everything was routine until the afternoon.

Sniper fire came across the area, followed by incoming rounds. Our grunts were returning fire but no fire mission was called. The Vietcong had used the cease-fire to move in towards our lines. Now they were dug in so deep and so close that we couldn't use bombs or artillery.

Sometimes we couldn't even fire the mortars, because the rounds would land too close to our men. The Vietcong move mainly at night and try to avoid an all-out attack.

It seems as though we keep kicking their asses, but we just never can get them all.

By this time Bob Soufo was getting short, a term used quite a bit for the guys leaving this country real soon. The word had come down that Bob would be leaving by chopper right from the operation. I was glad for him in so many ways, even though I was going to miss the hell out of him. Bob had been the platoon wireman my whole time over here. We went through a lot of shit together, including the time when he came back from R&R feeling really down and rejected. I guess this war in some ways cost him his marriage. He was only married a very short time when he left for Vietnam. While he was serving his country month after month, somebody else had occupied his wife's time. Bob spent most of his R&R trying to save his marriage. Nothing changed his wife's mind; she still insisted on a divorce, in order to be free to marry her playmate.

This tore Bob up badly because he really loved her. I was able to help Bob when he got back by just being a true-to-life buddy. Now I'm able to see Bob leave this country in a good frame of mind.

I remember when Bob came back from R&R and told me he had been home with his wife. I couldn't believe him. All that time he was gone, I thought he was having a ball in Hawaii. He definitely took a big chance. When he arrived in Hawaii, he grabbed the first plane to California. If Bob had been caught, they would have thrown the book at him.

The tenth day in the bush came and Bob and I were together constantly. We talked a lot about what he was going to do back in the States. I saw that Bob was more nervous now than before. I guess it happens to everybody when they get really close to leaving.

Up until now, all of our patrols had been around the DMZ. I got the word that we would be heading toward a place called An Dinh. It had been a while since I wrote a letter home, so I managed to get one done before we pulled out. In the letter I mentioned the fact that Bob wouldn't be going with me this time. He leaves tomorrow for Dong Ha.

I also told my mother to tell my Aunt Ann that this sweep is for her. Sweep is a term used to describe a move across an area, or a move to another area.

After some fifteen days in the bush, the four mortar guns had accumulated many dud rounds. Since we never leave anything behind for the Vietcong to play with, the rounds had to be blown. My squad acted as security outside the perimeter until all the dud rounds were safely blown.

When we did move out, we humped 2,000 meters before we settled in for the night.

Again, the gun pit was dug first, and then we built our hooches.

On January 13, the Vietcong threw mortars at us. There were no casualties in the mortar platoon, but there were some slight casualties with the grunts.

On the fourteenth of January, a section meeting was called. At the meeting I was handed my warrant for lance corporal. It went into effect as of January 1, and the warrant made it offical. The warrant, along with the recommendation in my record book, meant corporal stripes wouldn't be far off.

Toward evening we had hot chow flown in to us.

The next morning made our twentieth day in the bush. The morale of the men was low, as well as the level of supplies. We were told that any day now, our mail and beer and soda rations would be coming in. The C-rations we had would last a little bit longer. The more we stayed in the bush, the more of a strain the men had to deal with. All we knew from day to day was that we were still heading south. Seven of our men had been taken back to Dong Ha with blisters and open sores on their feet. Only one man was from my squad.

It wasn't until the twenty-second day of operation that I ran into some bad luck. We had been on the move all day, and toward sunset, while we were crossing a river, my foot slipped between two boulders, and I smashed my ankle. Later that evening, when I got a chance to get my boots off, I didn't like what I saw. Neither did the corpsman. The ankle was badly swollen, and I had the feeling from the corpsman that if I pushed the issue, I could probably get the hell out of here. It was a tempting thought, especially because of what happened a few days ago. However, the stupid pride I had made me want to stay with the platoon. If I was to miss an operation, it wouldn't be for something as minor as this.

I had been carrying a Vietcong aiming stake around with me, and it really came in handy now. I kept my weight off the foot as much as possible, and even though I limped around for a while, I was able to pull my share of the load. The aiming stake I mentioned was found by our section leader on Operation Hickory. The Vietcong use them when firing their mortars. At that time the section leader gave the stake to the senior man, and it was passed down everytime somebody left for home. When Bob left, I was the next one to carry it.

A couple of more days passed before our mail caught up to us. One of the letters I received was from Joe. He was also one of the fellows who was wounded badly on

July 25. Like Kincannon, he was now home and doing okay. By this time I had received a letter from all the fellows that were wounded the night Bruce was killed. Their wounds may be completely healed someday, but the scars and bad memories will be with them a lifetime.

Sunday, the twenty-first of January, was here, and the lieutenant told the squad leaders that as soon as possible we would catch choppers back to a place called Camp Carroll. There would be no replacements joining us this time, but at least we could get hot chow, hot showers, and a decent night's sleep.

We didn't move anywhere on the twenty-first, because we called for air support and for one reason or another couldn't get any. The same damn evening the Vietcong hit us with mortars and artillery. It lasted a few hours. When we did move out, we went a little over 2,000 meters more to a place near Phu Oc. We put the guns up first thing, and started digging our fighting holes. I stood lines with Frank that night, and we had the feeling that the Vietcong were wanting us to catch up to them.

On the twenty-ninth day of the operation, choppers came for us, but not until after we put a full exhausting day in. Again we left the bush, not knowing what the hell was accomplished. When we arrived at Camp Carroll, it was late. We still managed to get some hot chow, followed by a quiet night's rest. As for the hot showers, we would have to wait for a new day.

Since none of us could predict what tomorrow would bring, it didn't do a bit of good to worry about it. We just made the best of where we were.

After all, it wasn't every day we had the army watching over us. The night passed over, and it was one day closer to going home.

For most of us, it was easy getting up at 0600, especially when you knew there was more hot chow waiting. Hot showers for everybody was the very next thing on the list, but before we finished our breakfast the lieutenant passed the word to us to have our men get their packs ready. We were going back in the bush again, and real soon. There wouldn't be any showers today, and tomorrow it might not matter.

This time the choppers were waiting for us. Four gun ships would be flying alongside. Somebody had decided to call this Operation Lancaster II. Who knows, we might have been on Lancaster I and didn't even know it.

The choppers dropped us off in a valley, a nice peaceful valley. It wasn't far from where we were a few days ago. Evidently, Vietcong activity was spotted, and that's why we were back out in the bush. We had time to dig trenches before the Vietcong threw their artillery at us. This peaceful valley became a hot spot real fast.

After being hit with Vietcong artillery all night, the platoon commander passed along the word that we would be moving to the top of a nearby hill the first chance we got. It was Friday, January 26, and our casualties were still few. Our mortar platoon reached the hill and we dug in real well, perched on top. The grunt companies had dug in at the base of the hill, and two companies were midway up. All eight of our mortar guns were set up and ready for any fire missions. All four sides were covered with marines.

Nobody knew why we decided to set up on a hill, especially one we didn't have to clear Vietcong off first The hill was loaded with trees, and had narrow walkways cleared away and a main road in the center of the hill. It was easy to see the hill hadn't been used in a while, but the Vietcong had used this place before.

The day was quiet, but as soon as it got dark Charlie

moved in. All hell broke loose. Sniper fire came from the trees, but most of the fighting came from the base of the hill. Hour after hour the fighting went on. The night was pitch black, which didn't help things a bit.

When the fire missions were called, only four guns were able to respond. The other four guns were out of action.

Sniper fire was keeping some of the men pinned down.

One of the guns out of action was in my squad. Two of my men were pinned down by snipers; another one of my men was standing lines with the grunts. This left me with Pearce and Sodo. We were told to hold our positions, and while we were in our holes, hearing the screams of some of the grunts, I started wondering if any of us would make it until morning.

The Vietcong were playing an entirely different game. Instead of running from us, Charlie was now coming for us.

The morning did come, and we were certain things would ease up a little. Nobody knew during the night how many Vietcong we were fighting, but from the information that was gathered, it seems we stumbled onto a Vietcong regiment. Our casualty toll was climbing. Hunt from Gun Three was killed. Also from Gun Three was Tom, suffering with a stomach wound. Our corpsman was cut down trying to help the wounded. Our ammo was running low, but the main concern was to get our wounded off this hill. The colonel was taking charge himself, getting as many of the wounded men down to the landing zone for the medivac choppers. He needed some men to secure one of the walkways leading from the road. When he asked my section leader to spare some men, my squad was elected. The location we were in, men were getting a little scarce. Sodo, Pearce, and myself would have to be enough for the colonel. Our orders were to wait until the colonel gave the word to start down. Sodo was holding up okay under all this, but I was worried whether or not Pearce would make it. Sodo was from the Bronx, quiet, but cool. Pearce was a farm boy from Iowa, and this was the first time he saw any action. I asked him if he was okay, and he said yes, but real scared. The only thing I was able to say to him was something I remembered back in training. I told him to stay close to me or Sodo. Try not to get separated, and everything will probably fall into place. I told him to look at my hands. They were sweaty and shaky. "It's almost over for me," I said, "I'm almost going home, and I'm still as scared as you. I just don't intend to have it end for me now, not when it's almost over."

I didn't know if what I was saying was helping me or him. I was watching the colonel for the signal, but I glanced back and said to Pearce, "Do you know what I mean?"

I couldn't wait for his reply; it was time to move. The further down the hill we went, the noisier it got. Over eleven months in this paradise, and I never had the misfortune of walking as a point man until today. A point man is somebody who's first in line or the first one out.

(In almost all cases, the Vietcong try to carry their dead off, so that it's hard for us to ever get an accurate body count. I'm sure they also have a religious reason for this.) We were about halfway to a clearing where the colonel was taking the wounded through when I spotted a Vietcong lying in the road. My job was to make sure he was really dead. With my M-16 pointed at his head, I got a closer look. I had seen enough to convince me. Flies had started in on the open wound, and hundreds more were flying in and around his mouth. As we got near the base of the hill, the medivac choppers were coming in to land. The Vietcong wanted these babies bad, but the grunts were doing a damn good job keeping them off the wounded men.

Sodo, Pearce, and I joined in with the grunts in chasing after Charlie. There was so much confusion going on. It was hard enough just keeping from getting shot, without having to worry about staying together. From where I was, I couldn't see Pearce or Sodo, but I was sure they would head back to the top of the hill. For now, most of our critically wounded men had been taken out. My thoughts were on getting back to my buddies. I started back in the same direction as we came down, but didn't get very far.

When I heard the Vietcong open up with their rifles, I landed behind a few trees. I spotted two of them, but they were staying right where they were. They weren't coming after me, and I was getting used to where I was lying. I was breathing loud, but not so loud that I couldn't hear what was coming up behind me. I rolled over on my back, with my finger resting on the trigger. It was the damn lieutenant and I almost shot his head off. He was as surprised as I was but damn glad it was me. He told me to cover him on the way back to the top. When we did make the move, the lieutenant was really stepping out. We stopped only once, just before we reached an open area. After a breather, we made it across and then back to the platoon. The lieutenant passed the word that the platoon would be going down all at once just before dark. Sodo and Pearce had made it back okay, and they had done very well.

We were only a few hours away from darkness, and I was starting to have trouble with my stomach. The pains buckled me over several times, and I had a fever coming on. I knew that once we got off this hill, we would probably head back towards Camp Carroll for supplies. Then I could get checked at the battalion aid station.

Most of the fighting was still going on at the base of the hill, but we now had two squads of grunts strung out on both sides of the main path.

Before we started down, we gathered the fallen marines and carried them in ponchos. Nobody was going to be left for the Vietcong. I'm sure Charlie would have wanted us on top of that hill another night, because that's when they are at their best.

We fought our way in the direction of the road, chasing the Vietcong back into the underbrush and trees. I was burning up with a fever by now and could hardly hold myself up. I had one magazine of ammo left and hoped it would be enough.

When we got near the road, we could see the trucks. It was the army from Camp Carroll.

I was only about fifty feet from the trucks when I dropped to my knees and puked. Some of the fellows I rode back with were grateful for that.

When the trucks pulled in, I was helped over to the aid station. The corpsman checked me over and found my leg swollen with two marks on it. I had a bad infection and spent three days getting rid of it. He said something had bitten me. It was either a snake or a spider.

This was the second damn time one of those creatures had gotten away from me, and it was the third time I had been really sick. The whole time I was in Vietnam, I never weighed more than 151 pounds.

During the three days at the aid station, I managed to get a relaxing hot shower. The showers were just outside, and it was great not having to go very far. It was the first shower for me in over a month.

I had plenty of rest and I was going back to the squad. Even though I had to take pills and medicine for about another week, I was really feeling well.

The squad had been in good hands while I was gone. Fistler was next in line for squad leader, and he knew his job well.

I had a little over thirty days left now, and as far as the sergeant was concerned, I could be an extra man. He told me to relax and wait for my orders to Dong Ha. I helped Fistler from time to time and sat in on all the meetings. It was brought out that one mortar section would be staying at Camp Carroll.

The other three sections would be split up and attached to each of the grunt companies. The third section would be the first one to pull out. Their destination was Gho Lin. The fourth section was going to Camlo Bridge, and our section was headed back to Cam Lo Hill.

Staying at Camp Carroll was good for the men. The last operation had been a rough one, and the latest news we had was that our division had killed nearly 500 Vietcong. As for the men we lost or were wounded, none of us cared to know.

It was the seventeenth of February when we caught the trucks for Cam Lo Hill. The time was 1630. After the guns were set up, a schedule was made for FDC watch. I took my turn at standing watch and helped with all the fire missions. I was treated like a short-timer, which felt good. It meant I was going home.

I wanted to keep busy, because the trouble came when I tried to relax. Twelve months over here played hell on my nerves, and I was always on edge. It was still too early to go back and wait in Dong Ha for my orders, but I wasn't that anxious to leave my section anyway.

The word had gone around that in Dong Ha, the way things were being run were just a little bit too petty. The officers expected your boots shined and your brass polished. The short-timers were also expected to police the area, along with loads and loads of working parties.

101

Now I wanted to leave this country, and leave it fast. But by staying with my section as long as possible, I would be able to miss some of that stuff going on in Dong Ha.

I also knew that if the section moved out before my orders came in, I would have to make the decision whether to go with them or be sent back to Dong Ha.

Friday, February twenty-third came, and it seemed like a great day to throw a football around. We got together a game, and after it broke up, everybody got involved in throwing clogs of dirt around. It was another one of many things we did to keep our minds off this place.

I had the night off from FDC watch, but I gave Pete a break and took his watch from 2000 hours to 2100 hours. It was a good chance for me to write a letter. The same night, or actually very early the next morning, I had trouble sleeping, so I fired H and I's for one of the fellows from 0100 to 0300.

On the twenty-sixth day of February, Fistler was picked to go to Dong Ha for some of the things the squad needed. Before he left, he asked if there was anything I needed. I told him I needed only one thing: a set of orders saying I could go home.

While he was gone, I was left in charge again. Art and Gary were picked to fire H and I's from 0400 to 0700. I kept them company.

The next night, after evening chow, our new corpsman got together with Bob Roman and a marine that was born and raised in Hawaii. They started playing guitars, and they really sounded good. We also found out that Gary and Don could play the guitar. Don was our new section leader. He was from Nashville, Tennessee and was well liked.

It wasn't until February twenty-ninth that we finally had a fire mission where we actually knew what we were trying to hit. It was a Vietnam artillery piece. It was confirmed later by the grunts that we had knocked it out and killed two Vietcong.

March 1 was payday. I received $190. March 2 marked our fifteenth day back at Cam Lo Hill. The lieutenant inspected the rifles and pistols. By this time I had the feeling that the section wouldn't be pulling out, at least while I was still here. It was easy to see that the Vietcong activity wasn't as heavy in this area as it was a year ago.

A few more days passed, and there was still no word about my orders.

I knew it would have to be any day now because I was approaching my thirteenth month in this country. I worried more and more every day, wondering if my luck would hold out.

I wasn't getting much mail now, because I had written to tell everybody when I would be leaving. I didn't want my mail or packages taking three months to catch up to me.

The fellows were getting their R & R right on schedule. One marine would come back, and the next one was ready to leave.

Fistler had been transferred to another squad, and Vick took his place.

On March 8 I cleaned my weapon for what I hoped would be the last time. The lieutenant was going to let me go back on the next convoy.

I guess I was making him nervous now. When he told me the news and wished me good luck, chills ran through me. I knew when I left with the convoy, I might never see any of these fellows again. I loved some of these guys like brothers, which was the only good thing about the whole damn war. As true as this was, I wasn't going to ask to stay this time. I was ready, in more ways than one.

I had to wait for a convoy from Dong Ha, and it wasn't

103

until March eleventh that one arrived. It had been raining for days, and the mud was getting thicker all the time. The word had reached me that Wison from the third section was already in Dong Ha. He was waiting to see me. I was also told that there was a flight leaving for Da Nang on March 18 and that I would probably be on it. This was great to hear, but I wasn't going to make any bets.

On March 12 I was on the convoy when it rolled out of Cam Lo hill. It was 11:30 in the morning.

It was still raining when I got to Dong Ha. I checked in as soon as I could, and then went to the storage area to find my seabag. When I got back to the main area, Wison had saved me a cot next to his.

We did all our checking out together over the next few days and it was the same procedure as it was a year earlier. The only difference was that there were six of us walking around together last year.

If someone was keeping a score card on the six of us, it might have looked like this:

1—killed in action
1—wounded from enemy mortar
1—injured in accident
1—AWOL
2—unhurt

I met John on his way back from R&R, but we didn't have much time to get together. I was in the process of checking out, and he had to get back to the section. I told him to take care, and also to tell the fellows that I'm going to make it after all.

Wison and I were only stuck on a working party twice. Once was on March 14, when we were needed to fill sandbags. That lasted all day. The other time was yester-

104

day. We were sent over to the transit area to help build a bunker.

We got relieved at 1400 and were told to get a haircut and make a PX call.

It was March 16, when I got another check. I made $95, and it was the last time I got paid in Vietnam. The books were cleared on me, and my total earnings in Charlie's paradise came to $2,094, in American dollars. Low wages for a high-cost war.

Later in the day we turned in our weapons and went over to the aid station to get a shot. This shot was to be the first one of many more we would have to get in Okinawa.

When we picked up our first set of orders at the end of the day, we got the word that we would be leaving on the first flight in the morning for Da Nang. It was one day earlier than we had expected, and it was the best news I had heard in a long, long time.

The morning came, and the plane was serviced and ready to go. We were there waiting and ready to go also. Somehow, the whole idea of us leaving this country wasn't quite a reality. We were not out of the country yet. There was still one more night in Da Nang to make it through.

Some of us fellows went to the China Beach area to take one more look around. We stopped at the club and had a few, before returning to the huts. Tomorrow, if and when it comes, will be a glorious day.

Epilogue

When the morning arrived, it certainly was a glorious day for me and a number of other marines who were finally leaving. We had done our share of the fighting and had survived our tour of duty.

In the early morning of March 18, 1968, I, Lance Cpl. Mike Vichelli, left Charlie's paradise by way of Continental Airlines.

When the plane was safely in the air, only then was I convinced that it had become a reality.

As I glanced around the plane, I wondered if I would be able to adjust to some of the things back home. I was taking back with me a lot of bad memories and a few bad habits. My nerves were practically gone, and when I got excited, a slight stuttering occured. Compared to some of my buddies, this was nothing at all.

My true Vietnam experience ended there on the plane ride, and though there are many people who know all too well what became of me, there are many many more who don't.

Some of the questions a reader might ponder are as follows:

1. Did Vichelli stay in the marine corps, and if so, did he ever have to go back to Vietnam?
2. After his discharge, did he adjust to civilian life?
3. Did he ever get married and, if so, how many children did he have?
4. Did he end up in any VA hospitals for nervous disorders or alcoholism?

107

5. Is he still living today and, if so, in what state?
6. How old was Vichelli when he wrote the book?
7. What was his discharge date and his rank at that time?
8. Did the war leave him with bitter feelings?
9. What was his religious background?
10. Was he ever able to forget his experience?

The answers to some of these questions may never come out or be told, unless I decide to tell it like it is, one more time.